AIR CAMPAIGN

OPERATION *RO-GO* 1943

Japanese air power tackles the Bougainville landings

MICHAEL JOHN CLARINGBOULD | ILLUSTRATED BY JIM LAURIER

OSPREY PUBLISHING
Bloomsbury Publishing Plc
Kemp House, Chawley Park, Cumnor Hill, Oxford OX2 9PH, UK
29 Earlsfort Terrace, Dublin 2, Ireland
1385 Broadway, 5th Floor, New York, NY 10018, USA
E-mail: info@ospreypublishing.com
www.ospreypublishing.com

OSPREY is a trademark of Osprey Publishing Ltd

First published in Great Britain in 2023

A catalogue record for this book is available from the British Library.

ISBN: PB 9781472855572; eBook 9781472855565;
ePDF 9781472855589; XML 9781472855596

23 24 25 26 27 10 9 8 7 6 5 4 3 2 1

Maps by bounford.com
Diagrams by Adam Tooby
3D BEVs by Paul Kime
Index by Fionbar Lyons
Typeset by PDQ Digital Media Solutions, Bungay, UK
Printed and bound in India by Replika Press Private Ltd.

Osprey Publishing supports the Woodland Trust, the UK's leading woodland conservation
charity.

To find out more about our authors and books visit www.ospreypublishing.com. Here
you will find extracts, author interviews, details of forthcoming events and the option to
sign up for our newsletter.

Photo on title page: see page 19.
Author's note
All Japanese names are surname first.
All photos from author's private collection.
Ku is used as an abbreviation for Kokutai.

CONTENTS

INTRODUCTION

A line-up of 204 Ku Zero-sen at Lakunai with the "Mother" volcano in the background.

Operation *Ro-Go* is one of history's paradoxes. From the outset its objective was to slow American advances primarily in New Guinea but also the Solomons. The Imperial Japanese Navy initiative was planned with minimal collaboration with the Imperial Army, but things went awry very quickly. Its offensive ambitions coincidentally dovetailed with the commencement of the Allied northern Solomons campaign. There was prevarication leading up to the launch of the operation, and for good reason.

Just as Operation *Ro-Go* was about to be implemented, an Allied landing on Mono and Stirling Islands just southwest of Bougainville by the New Zealand forces on October 27, 1943 saw both islands occupied and secured. In response, Commander of the Combined Fleet, Admiral Koga Mineichi, authorized Operation *Ro-Go* to proceed on October 28, 1943. The term "*Ro-Go Sakusen*" (ろ号作戦 in Hiragana and Kanji) derives from "*sakusen*," meaning "operation," "*Ro*" from the respective Hiragana letter, and "*Go*" being a number/letter designator. The carrier-based contingent would fly to Rabaul from Truk on November 1 and return on November 13. For the Allies, however, the small-scale landings were just a precursor to the main game, a major landing at Torokina on Bougainville planned for November 1. The date coincided with the same day the First Carrier Division aircraft ferried themselves down to Rabaul from Truk.

It is important to stress that both sides of the campaign were adversely affected by weather throughout. The characteristic wet season was worse than usual, and contested areas and the flightpaths to targets were regularly battered by frontal systems with attendant squall lines, rain, and poor visibility. Thus the timing and execution of strikes was often dictated more by weather considerations than strategic or operational ones. Before leaving Truk, the crews were told that their primary duty would be to attack enemy shipping, check enemy counteroffensives, and destroy enemy surface units.

However, Operation *Ro-Go*'s objectives abruptly switched to striking the Torokina landing area and the task force of ships which supported it. It is impossible to separate Operation *Ro-Go* from a series of naval battles that ensued over forthcoming weeks, as the outcomes of these confrontations much dictated its air movements. Added to the mix was a task force of cruisers and destroyers led by Vice Admiral Omori Sentaro which steamed from Rabaul on November 1 to destroy the American ships offshore Torokina. Six RAAF (Royal Australian Air Force) No. 8 Squadron Beauforts armed with torpedoes swept their likely path toward Bougainville but failed to find Omori's ships. Then, that evening, a USN (US Navy) task force under Rear Admiral Aaron Merrill attacked around 50 miles north of the Torokina beachhead. A resultant two-hour furious naval battle saw off the Japanese ships which retired back to Rabaul.

The following day, November 2, the carrier aircraft from Truk had an opportunity to launch their first strike at the beachhead. The futile result was a loss of six dive-bombers. Then, when preparing for a second strike after their return, they became tangled with the biggest Fifth Air Force strike against Rabaul. It was hard to determine which side was more surprised at the size of each other's aerial forces, but suddenly Operation *Ro-Go*'s air power was being worn down by costly defensive action. Then, USN carrier aircraft hit Rabaul with substantive strikes on November 5 and 11. While damage to shipping was substantial, the real success of these raids was that the threat to the ongoing northern Solomons operations was allayed when all IJN (Imperial Japanese Navy) cruisers were withdrawn back to Truk.

The origins of Operation *Ro-Go* were built on the alleged success of its predecessor, Operation *I*, also known in Western references as Operation *I-Go*. Back in April 1943 former Commander of the Combined Fleet, Admiral Yamamoto Isoroku, had authorized Operation *I*. IJN staff officers at Rabaul optimistically had assessed the operation a success; however, the reality was it had barely dinted Allied efforts. A summary conference of Operation *I* was held in Rabaul on April 16, 1943 following Yamamoto's declaration of the operation's successful conclusion. Nonetheless, 11th Air Fleet and carrier division staff officers both expressed concern over "severe aircraft losses," for the operation's four strikes had cost 45 Japanese aircraft, both land and carrier-based. The meeting concluded with the pessimistic realization that the Japanese were faced with expanding enemy air power they could not stop. Since the conference, the Japanese had unsuccessfully attempted to hold the line throughout the central Solomons and New Guinea via air power. The growing disparity between Japanese and Allied air power had widened more quickly than the Japanese anticipated throughout 1943.

Several Japanese magazines published articles and photos from Operation *Ro-Go* The map on the cover of this one labels, among others, the locations of Torokina, Mono Island, and the Shortlands in Katakana. The magazine promises its readers an exciting update on a "decisive battle."

An RNZAF P-40M is towed to its hardstand at Piva Yoke in early 1944.

Now, in late 1943, new Allied technology, combined with immense materiel from the base at Espiritu Santo, was making headway toward Rabaul. Following the loss of Yamamoto over Bougainville on April 18, 1943 to USAAF (US Army Air Forces) fighter interception, Admiral Koga Mineichi was appointed replacement Commander of the Combined Fleet. Koga, who shared similar misgivings with his predecessor regarding war with the United States, nevertheless attempted to rejuvenate the IJN. He restructured the Combined Fleet into task forces centered around aircraft carriers, in a sense replicating the doctrine of the USN. Koga also saw advantages of land-based air

An RNZAF P-40 taxies at Torokina in late December 1943, by which time most of the complex had been finished.

power working together with carrier-based aircraft. In planning another major strike in the "South Seas," Koga knew that morale in the carrier units was superior to that of their land-based counterparts. Furthermore, the carrier pilots were healthier, and their attitude more aggressive.

The high losses sustained during Operation *I* did not deter Koga's resolve that another major strike could blunt Allied encroachment upon Rabaul. Thus, a plan was initially set in motion for late October 1943. Koga, who possessed a realist's strategic mind, was under no illusion that the IJN could wipe out Allied air power. Instead, he intended that a major offensive would seriously impede it. This would allow sufficient breathing space to consolidate Rabaul as a stronghold. To do this, Koga needed the extra firepower afforded by carrier aviation and approached Admiral Ozawa Jisaburo to borrow the air power of the three carriers of the First Carrier Division – *Zuikaku*, *Shokaku*, and *Zuiho*. Ozawa's approval added 173 aircraft to the operation. The contingent would be land-based, and spread over three Rabaul airfields of Rapopo, Lakunai, and Vunakanau.

Back in May 1943, *Zuikaku* and *Zuiho* had replenished their air groups at Truk, but the influx of green cadre contained many inexperienced pilots. The carrier air units still retained a limited hard core of battle-experienced division officers, but in general the major proportion of flight leaders lacked gravitas. Indicative of the wanting situation is the appointment of several junior officers around this time to key operational positions. Air staff officer for the Second Carrier Division at the time, Lieutenant Commander Okumiya Masatake, observed post-war, "We were required to train many lieutenants directly out of flying school. These men had barely thirty days' carrier training . . . not only did we fear for the safety of these new pilots in combat, but many had considerable difficulty in merely properly flying their fighters and bombers."

A total of 173 aircraft from the First Carrier Division flew to Rabaul on November 1, comprising 82 Zero-sen, 45 Val dive-bombers, 40 Kate torpedo bombers, and six Judy reconnaissance aircraft. At Rabaul they joined the land-based units of Admiral Kusaka Jinichi's 11th Air Fleet.

Central to the unfolding of Operation *Ro-Go* was the situation in Bougainville. When the Japanese evacuated Guadalcanal in February 1943, they transferred their troops to the southern part of Bougainville, centered on Buin and the Shortland Islands. The 17th Army commander, Lieutenant General Hyakutake Haruyoshi, established his headquarters on Erventa Island, just offshore Buin, and then transformed Bougainville into a defensive stronghold. Confident he could hold Bougainville at any cost, Hyakutake, a dominating personality, concentrated his forces around Buka, Kieta, and the Buin/Shortlands area in the belief that these locations were where the Allies most likely would attack. Reinforcements from Rabaul consolidated Hyakutake's ambitions, and when Operation *Ro-Go* commenced there were around 40,000 IJA troops and 22,900 IJN personnel stationed on Bougainville. In the first few days of Operation *Ro-Go*, the Allied landing at Torokina placed 14,321 US troops ashore, their primary object to secure land for an airfield complex. This area had not featured in Hyakutake's thinking, and the only Japanese forces defending the area were a forward observation post bolstered by an infantry detachment.

The IJN operational logs for Operation *Ro-Go* are highly detailed, and betray both losses and combat claims exponentially higher than that of Operation *I*. However, the Japanese made extravagant claims during Operation *Ro-Go*, comparable in hyperbole to those made by General George Kenney's Fifth Air Force during the October–November 1943 series of Rabaul air strikes. Following the major one of November 2, Kenney declared that Rabaul was annihilated and so suspended offensive aerial operations. In fact, the strike, while incurring limited damage to Japanese shipping, did not affect Japanese ambition at all. It unfolded on the second day of Operation *Ro-Go*, the US losses earning the nickname "Bloody Tuesday" among US airmen. In terms of numerical losses, the Fifth Air Force came off second best, a fact still not acknowledged in Western accounts today. Contrary to the elated American press articles about the raid, the Japanese were clear victors; the USAAF lost 11 Mitchells and nine Lightnings, a total of 20 aircraft.

Staff of Rabaul's *Kempetai* (military police) headquarters. The kanji on both vertical pillars reads "South Seas military detachment."

USAAF claims totaled 55 aerial kills, but Japanese operational records list only 14 Zeros lost to combat, a clear numerical victory for the Japanese.

With the withdrawal of the Fifth Air Force from the campaign, a direct threat suddenly appeared to the Torokina landing from IJN warships sent to Rabaul at short notice. This forced the USN to conduct two major carrier strikes against Rabaul shipping on November 5 and 11, and Operation *Ro-Go* switched to destroying the culprit US carriers.

Follow-on profligate claims made by Japanese aircrew against USN carrier task forces were mostly accepted at face value by Rabaul's staff officers, when in fact they were implausible to the extreme. Some of the overly optimistic assessments, especially those pertaining to shipping claims, can be attributed to aircrew inexperience and faulty intelligence assessment. However, there was more than that. Desperate circumstances allowed wishful thinking to influence assessments which, under ordinary circumstances, would have been dismissed. It would be interesting to know how much Admiral Koga himself believed the claims as presented.

Both Operations *I* and *Ro-Go* highlight an inherent weakness woven into Japanese air doctrine and strategy at the time. Both were based on the principle that a limited series of major air strikes could alter the balance of power within a theater. However, by late 1943 such an assumption was flawed in the face of massive Allied materiel superiority. To be fair, the concept had proved workable in the war's opening months; Pearl Harbor had crippled the US Pacific Fleet, and air superiority over the Philippines had been attained with a limited number of strikes. The March–April 1942 Indian Ocean carrier raid had cleared the British Royal Navy from the western Indian Ocean. However, these initiatives had triumphed because their adversaries lacked logistical supply lines and equipment. By 1943, the Allies had built sufficient supply chains to easily meet Japanese air power on equal terms, and quickly replace aircraft and shipping losses. In the face of all this, the IJN still clung to this previous strategy of decisive strikes to overwhelm the foe. Substantive follow-on action required was, for the Japanese, unsustainable.

However, there was no shortage of seasoned and realistic Japanese staff officers at Rabaul. By late 1943 it was apparent to this cadre of senior pragmatists that the IJN could no longer secure quick victories in the South Seas. Neither was Rabaul capable of winning the grinding battle of attrition which grew more arduous by the month. Regardless, as a matter of honor Rabaul refused to concede any leeway for defeat. Supported with Tokyo's imperator and political ambition, it kept hurling limited air power at burgeoning Allied resources. In the final analysis, Operation *Ro-Go* made negligible difference to Allied ambitions and progress in the northern Solomons campaign. A study of the campaign gives unique insight into an IJN increasingly on the back foot, a conservative and traditional military in the process of being overwhelmed both by technology and logistics. Inflexible IJN doctrine saw Rabaul's efforts repeatedly fail against an encroachment it could neither repel nor, in some cases, comprehend.

CHRONOLOGY

1942

January 23 The Japanese capture Rabaul, preparing Vunakanau and Lakunai airfields for use by land-based aircraft.

January 27 Lt Okamoto Harutoshi arrives at Rabaul leading a contingent of *Chitose* Ku A5M4 Claude fighters. These are the first land-based aircraft to arrive at Rabaul. Okamoto will return to Rabaul in 1943 as a tactician and *chutaicho*.

April 23 Brigadier General William Rose arrives at Espiritu Santo from Efate via a J2F-5 Duck amphibian. He heads "Task Force A," which will eventually build a mammoth logistics base for SOPAC (South Pacific Area) operations, including four major airfields, which will reach its zenith in late 1943.

August 7 US forces capture the Japanese airfield still under construction on Guadalcanal which the Japanese call "Runga" (later Henderson Field).

1943

February 20 US forces seize the Russell Islands unopposed and start building Pavuvu and Banika airfields.

April 7 First strike of Operation *I* launched against Guadalcanal.

April 28 MacArthur approves Operation *Elkton III*, which will bypass Rabaul; however, air strikes will continue to wear it down.

June 30 The Allies invade Rendova.

July 3 In the face of Allied advances, Japanese commanders confer at Munda to determine the future defense of the Solomons, presided over by Rear Admiral Ota Minoru, Commander No. 8 Special Naval Landing Force (SNLF).

August 14 Munda airfield becomes operational for Allied aircraft.

August 30 Tobera airfield becomes operational. During Operation *Ro-Go* its facilities, including cement runway and revetments, will be used by Zero-sen from 253 Ku and *Zuikaku*.

September 1 251 Ku is reclassified as a night-fighter unit equipped with the J1N1 Irving. Its remaining Zero-sen are dispersed between Rabaul's other fighter units.

September 6 The F6F Hellcat claims its first combat victory in the Solomons campaign.

October 12 Fifth Air Force begins a major air offensive to neutralize Rabaul. The first targets are Vunakanau, Rapopo, and Tobera airfields from both high and low altitudes.

October 18 Fifth Air Force launches its second major strike against Rabaul's airfields; however, bad weather prevents all but a 345th Bombardment Group B-25D strafer formation to get through.

October 18–21 Ballale and then Buin airfields are declared unserviceable by the Japanese.

October 27 New Zealand and US troops land on Mono Island.

October 28 Following weeks of deliberation, Admiral Koga Mineichi authorizes Operation *Ro-Go* to proceed.

October 31–November 1 USN ships shell Buka airfield and facilities on the Shortland Islands at night and early morning.

November 1 – morning Operation *Ro-Go* commences, with a total of 173 aircraft from the First Carrier Division flying the long distance from Truk to Rabaul. These include 82 Zero-sen, 45 Val dive-bombers, 40 Kate torpedo bombers, and six Judy reconnaissance aircraft.

Zero-sen 204 Ku pilot Lt (jg) Fukuda Sumio leads the operation's first strike, which is resisted by Allied fighters. Two dozen Zero-sen from 201 Ku, 20 from 204 Ku and eight Val dive-bombers from 582 Ku accompany a solitary 501 Ku Judy in combat.

The commencement of Operation *Cherry Blossom*, the Allied invasion of the Torokina beachhead on Bougainville. The objective is to build an airfield complex so that SOPAC fighters can reach Rabaul.

November 1 and 2 (night) IJN cruisers and destroyers attempt a counter-invasion at Torokina; however, they are defeated at the Battle of Empress Augusta Bay during a night action.

November 2 The IJN sends a strike force of 83 aircraft from Rabaul to strike US shipping offshore Torokina beachhead. The attackers are met by combined American and RNZAF (Royal New Zealand Air Force) fighters, and the attack causes minimal damage. Despite massive Allied claims, the Japanese lose only six Vals.

Following the return of the Japanese aircraft from their morning attack, Fifth Air Force strafers attack Simpson Harbour, sinking and damaging several warships. This prevents a major planned second Japanese strike against Bougainville. Over Rabaul the USAAF lose 20 aircraft to unexpectedly fierce resistance, which includes carrier-based Zero-sen which Allied intelligence did not know were there. The USAAF claim 55 aerial kills, but Japanese losses are confined to 14 Zeros.

November 3 Eight cruisers and four destroyers are sent from Truk to Rabaul to reinforce Japanese naval forces there.

A dogfight over Empress Augusta Bay sees an even score of two aircraft lost per side.

November 5 – morning USN carriers *Saratoga* and *Princeton* strike shipping in Simpson shortly after the Japanese naval reinforcements arrive there. The carriers launch a total of 97 aircraft: 52 F6F Hellcats, 23 TBF Avengers, and 22 SBD-5 Dauntless dive-bombers. Seven cruisers are damaged, preventing the Japanese from attempting a planned surface action that night against Bougainville.

November 5 – evening Kates conduct a torpedo attack against three small USN vessels, losing four. The IJN claims to sink one large and one medium aircraft carrier, along with two cruisers and two destroyers. The strike marks the biggest over-claim of Operation *Ro-Go*.

November 6 Jake floatplanes attack the Torokina landing area, inflicting minimal damage. Meanwhile, the IJA lands 21 barges near the mouth of the Laruma River, disgorging an estimated 400 troops, northwest of Torokina. The troops are resisted by US ground forces

A TBF-1 is serviced aboard a carrier.

and air support, in a series of actions which continue throughout November 7 and 8.

November 7 The Japanese 6th Division based at Buka starts advancing toward Torokina.

Four Fifth Air Force P-38s are shot down by defending Zero-sen over Rabaul, for no Japanese losses despite profligate US claims.

November 8 Renowned *Zuikaku* division officer and strike commander Lt Notomi Kenjiro goes MIA during combat.

November 8–9 A night shipping strike against USN cruisers offshore the Treasury Islands costs four Kates and eight Bettys.

A glitch in morale sees a long-planned RAAF night torpedo strike from Kiriwina of a dozen Beauforts reduced to three. Squadron Leader Owen Price is lost in the attack.

November 10–11 Five of 14 Kates are lost during a night strike against Torokina beachhead, including mission leader *Zuikaku* division officer Lt Miyao Usuru.

A Model 22 G4M1 Betty, identified by its spinners, about to depart on another mission.

November 11 – morning As a follow-on from the November 5 attack, USN aircraft from carriers *Essex*, *Bunker Hill*, *Independence*, *Saratoga*, and *Princeton* strike Rabaul at 0900hrs, sinking or damaging four Japanese warships.

November 11 – mid-afternoon A Japanese counterstrike of 76 aircraft against Task Group 50.3 centered upon carriers *Essex*, *Bunker Hill*, and *Independence* proves disastrous, with 37 aircraft shot down or lost. Heavy AA and Allied fighter interception sees little damage incurred by the targeted USN ships, marking the biggest Japanese loss for the entire operation.

November 11–12 (night) Two groups of Bettys fail to locate the retreating Task Group 50.3.

November 12 Admiral Koga orders the withdrawal of the majority of the surviving carrier aircraft back to Truk. Detachments from *Zuikaku* stay on in Rabaul until January 1944.

November 13 Surviving aircraft of First Carrier Division fly from Rabaul back to Truk. Koga declares the conclusion of Operation *Ro-Go*; however, IJN strikes continue against the Torokina beachhead and Mono Island using land-attackers from the 11th Air Fleet.

November 15 Twenty-six brand-new D3A2 Model 22 Vals from 552 Ku based in the Marshall Islands, led by group commander Captain Tanaka Yoshio, depart for Rabaul to reinforce its dive-bomber inventory.

December 17 The first major land-based fighter sweep over Rabaul conducted from Torokina.

1945
September 4 HMS *Vendetta* enters Simpson Harbour. A Japanese delegation led by 11th Air Fleet staff officer Captain Sanagi Takeshi boards to organize a formal surrender of all Japanese forces at Rabaul set two days hence.

September 6 The Japanese surrender at Rabaul, signed by General Imamura Hitoshi and Admiral Kusaka Jinichi.

1946
October The last Japanese POWs from Rabaul are repatriated back to Japan by ship. However, a key collective of POWs are retained for war crimes trials. Some of the convicted are hanged.

ATTACKER'S CAPABILITIES

Japan's success in Operation *Ro-Go* depended on having ample aircraft of the right type, adequate airfield infrastructure from which to conduct attacks, effective weapons and tactics, and the critical but elusive gift of trained aircrew with good morale. The Japanese forces involved could meet some of these conditions, but not all. In logistical terms, the addition of carrier-based air units to the operation was imperative, as Rabaul's land-based units were badly worn down at this stage of the war. However, this incorporation had its own dangers, as combining the two forces involved mixing differing morale and health benchmarks. Carrier division air staff officer, Lieutenant Commander Okumiya Masatake, who deployed to Rabaul after Operation *Ro-Go*, viewed the problem thus:

> I knew that the defeatist attitude prevailing at Rabaul would adversely affect my own staff. I had to take every step to prevent the lethargy affecting the land-based 26th Flotilla from being transmitted to my own group. Until I arrived at Rabaul we permitted the replacement staffs to work together with the groups being relieved. The overlapping duties permitted rapid familiarization with the procedures of the base.

The willpower so characteristic of the land-based aviation units when they first arrived at Rabaul had evaporated. The struggles of the past year and a half had cost the 11th Air Fleet most of its cadre of experienced aircrew. With each passing day of Operation *Ro-Go*, it becomes clear that there was a deliberate command decision to give priority to deployment of First Carrier Division resources rather than those of the 11th Air Fleet. There were numerous times when land-based units could have been used but were not. This is the marked difference to the operation's predecessor – Operation *I* – in which both land-based and carrier units shared an equal, proportionate responsibility.

Furthermore, the problem of crew inexperience was serious enough with land-based fighter pilots, but also applied to the Betty crews, some members of which had received only perfunctory training or, by late 1943, even none at all. A shortage of Betty crews

IJN officers inspect a nurses' parade at the Navy hospital located near Keravia village in a former plantation residence. The officer in the center is likely Rear Admiral Takata Jiro.

meant some missions were flown with as few as five crew instead of the standard complement of seven. Warrant Officer Yokoyama Kazuyoshi was a 751 Ku Betty observer, who was captured shortly after Operation *Ro-Go* and summarized the morale at Rabaul: "At Vunakanau we were all disgusted with the state of affairs which necessitated us being on the defensive. Japanese morale was founded on always taking the initiative and pressing forward. Everyone was hoping the tide would turn."

The disparity in morale between the carrier and land-based groups was exacerbated by a wide gap in their relative health too. Poor health was widespread throughout the land-based units at Rabaul. The entire Rabaul garrison had suffered declining health persistently since its arrival in early 1942. The most debilitating ailment was vivax malaria, and by the time of Operation *Ro-Go* one man out of five had suffered at least one bout. Furthermore, once contracted, the disease was difficult to manage, as once lodged it could not be eradicated. Other chronic diseases included diarrhea, respiratory disorders, tuberculosis, and worm-ridden kidney infection. Poor health impaired a pilot's ability to fly combat, especially given the demands of formation flying required for missions down to Bougainville and Empress Augusta Bay.

For the visiting carrier pilots, accustomed to regular rest and good food, their accommodation and conditions in Rabaul were a shock and denied them good repose. While officers above the rank of lieutenant were housed in wooden barracks two or three to a room, junior grade officers were accommodated in damp six- and four-man tents, while all other ranks slept in crowded tents which regularly housed eight or more men. The wet weather which attended their sojourn did not assist matters.

Each air group had its own medical unit; however, more seriously injured aircrew received adequate medical treatment at one of two IJN hospitals, depending on the severity of their injuries. The most serious were evacuated to Japan by Combined Fleet Mavis flying boats.

The 8th Fleet Navy Hospital built in 1909 by the German administration was located near Government House at Namanula, and was commanded by Captain Sekuzu Ei'ichi, who had previously served aboard cruiser *Isuzu* as ship's surgeon. The Navy hospital commanded by Rear Admiral Takata Jiro was located near Keravia village in a former plantation residence. Nonetheless, persistent Allied bombings had by this stage interrupted both hospitals' daily life, resulting in fatigue among the staff and depleted medical supplies. Civilian nurses from Japan attended both hospitals and were young; as an example, one administrative assistant when she arrived at Rabaul is manifested as 17 years old. The Japanese nursing cadre was evacuated back to Japan as Allied air raids became more intense. Their departure commenced shortly after the conclusion of Operation *Ro-Go*, with the final batch evacuated by the end of January 1944.

Airfields

Operation *Ro-Go* needed reliable and serviceable airfields. Although there were five around Rabaul, only three were used for the operation; in terms of importance these were Vunakanau, Lakunai, and Tobera. A considerable challenge was the dispersal of the carrier units between these airfields, and then the coordination of strike departures given their geographical distance apart. As a rule, all fighters and reconnaissance aircraft (including

151 Ku's Judys) were based at Lakunai, but there was an exception: Tobera was home to the Zero-sen of 253 Ku led by Commander Fukuda Taro. Tobera had a concrete runway and a limited number of revetments; however, Zuikaku's Zero-sen would base themselves here alongside 253 Ku throughout Operation *Ro-Go*.

Situated on a plateau to the west of Rabaul (termed "Rabaul West" or the "Upper Drome" by the Japanese), Vunakanau was located some 15 miles inland and to the southwest of the township of Rabaul. It had become a well-developed and sprawling base, with bomber and fighter revetments, generators, and maintenance facilities. Its cantonment areas housed more than a million tons of fuel and oil, along with secure ordnance storage with adequate supplies of bombs, ammunition, and torpedoes. Its main runway was concrete; however, rainy periods turned the taxiways into a quagmire. All bomber operations would be based here, including the Val and Judy dive-bombers and the carrier-based Kate attack bombers.

Lakunai ("Rabaul East" or "Rabaul Lower") permitted takeoff from either direction, and the view of Tavurvur volcano to the southeast was distinctive and imposing. In 1942, a construction unit had bulldozed a 1,500 x 100m runway from the former RAAF grass airfield, but a depression in the middle made it unsafe for bombers with full loads. Even before the carrier aircraft arrived, Lakunai faced the logistic challenges of maintaining and launching the Zero-sen inventories of 201 Ku led by Commander Nakano Chujiro and 204 Ku led by Commander Shibata Takeo. The Zero-sen contingents of *Zuiho* and *Shokaku* would soon join them.

IJN engineers inspect projectile damage to the wing of a Model 22 Zero-sen at Vunakanau after an air battle over Rabaul in late 1943.

BELOW
Antiaircraft radar fire control installed in September 1943 not far from Vunakanau, photographed here in October 1943 during a low-level strike. The equipment did not perform well, however, and within a month fell unserviceable largely due to high humidity and heat. The two huts at the rear surrounded by four poles each are associated direction finders.

Radar

At the time of Operation *Ro-Go* Rabaul had seven radar sets, which fell under the control of IJN commander Doi Yasumi, Chief Gunnery Officer at Rabaul, and coincidentally an early morning horse-riding partner of Admiral Kusaka Jinichi. Other sets were located on the plateau area behind Vunakanau, and one at Raluana Point. A set at Cape St. George could theoretically warn of approaching aircraft at a distance up to 100km (62 miles); however, these sets provided no warning of the two USN raids of November 5 and 11. Rabaul also had antiaircraft radar fire control equipment, the first of which had been installed in September 1943. The first Japanese equipment of its kind, it did not perform well, and within a month had fallen unserviceable. The USN approach path for the carrier-launched November 5 and 11 raids also bypassed several Japanese observation posts along the Solomons chain, including those on Choiseul and the Shortlands.

OPPOSITE RABAUL/TRUK/BOUGAINVILLE AREA AND JAPANESE MOVEMENT OF AIR POWER

Movements of the Allied and Japanese aerial forces throughout the campaign, excluding USN aerial forces. The delivery flight to Rabaul from Truk for the First Carrier Division was nearly 800 miles and was a feat of long-distance navigation in itself for the smaller types of aircraft.

Torpedoes

The Type 91 aerial torpedo was commonly used by both the Betty and Kate units throughout Operation *Ro-Go*. It was an eight-fin torpedo with anti-roll flippers, able to be launched up to 300 knots and carrying a 235kg (518lb) warhead. On the Kates, where the weapon was slung underneath the fuselage, wooden fins were attached to stabilize the torpedo while airborne. The wooden fins were slid forward on grooves onto the metal fins. A wooden block was inserted into a leading-edge groove on each wooden fin, which retained them in flight. When the torpedo struck the water, the wooden fins broke off, leaving the metal fins to assume the guidance to target.

Floatplanes

The floatplanes of 938 Ku (Commander Terai Kunizo) and 958 Ku (Captain I'ida Rinjuro) were scattered between Rabaul's Malaguna Bay and Matapai floatplane bases, the Shortland Islands, Kavieng, and Buka. All these anchorages held good facilities and secure moorings. Although both units were equipped with the E13A1 Jake and F1M2 Pete, it was the former type which was primarily deployed during Operation *Ro-Go* due to its extended range as a reconnaissance platform. It also often carried a pair of 60kg (132lb) bombs, mostly ineffectual against shipping and land targets. However, its reliability and first-rate performance enabled it to perform multiple medium-range tasks, including patrols, night attacks, liaison, rescues, and reconnaissance.

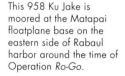

This 958 Ku Jake is moored at the Matapai floatplane base on the eastern side of Rabaul harbor around the time of Operation *Ro-Go*.

938 Ku had been established in April 1943 by combining the floatplanes of *Chitose*, *Kunikawa Maru*, and *Kamikawa Maru*. However, throughout the July–September 1943 Rendova campaign, the group had suffered major losses, and by the time of Operation *Ro-Go* many of its crews were fresh and inexperienced replacements from Japan.

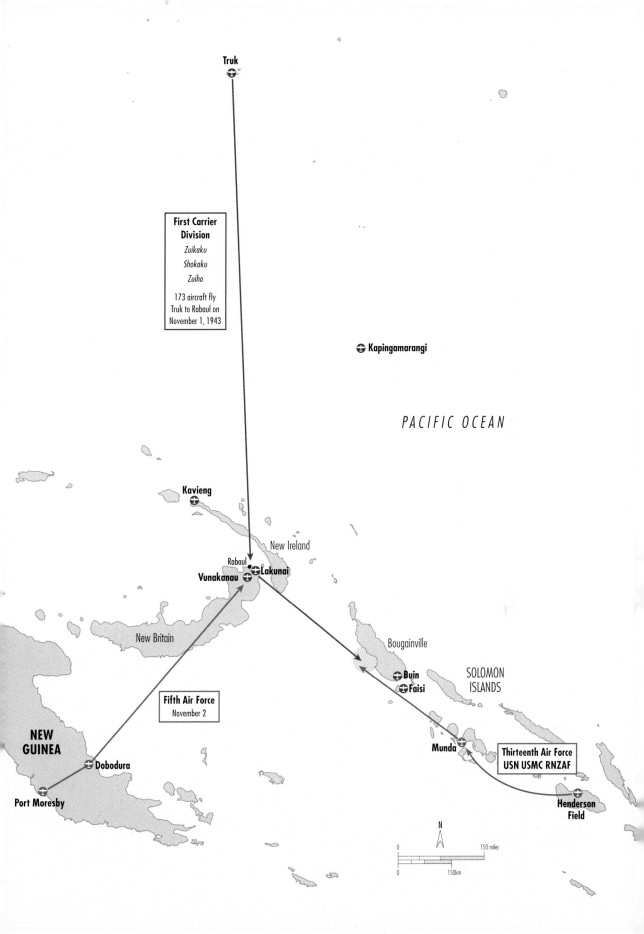

Truk

First Carrier Division
Zuikaku
Shokaku
Zuiho

173 aircraft fly
Truk to Rabaul on
November 1, 1943

⊕ **Kapingamarangi**

PACIFIC OCEAN

Kavieng

New Ireland

Rabaul
Vunakanau ⊕ ⊕ **Lakunai**

New Britain

Bougainville

Buin
Faisi

SOLOMON
ISLANDS

Fifth Air Force
November 2

**NEW
GUINEA**

Dobodura

Munda

**Thirteenth Air Force
USN USMC RNZAF**

Port Moresby

**Henderson
Field**

N

0   150 miles

0   150km

Assigned to the 8th Fleet, its sister air group 958 Ku had been established at Rabaul on December 1, 1942 and was classified as a fleet support unit with the role of anti-submarine patrol and reconnaissance. A mid-June 1943 report lists the numerous woes of the unit's worn and depleted inventory, and perhaps more importantly, rated only one-third of its crews as "A" or above in capability. The report concludes that a shortage of operational leadership was impairing operations.

Betty

The IJN backbone attack bomber and successor to the Nell, the G4M1 Betty had experienced a disastrous loss rate over Guadalcanal from mid-1942 onwards, especially during low-level shipping strikes. While one of its strengths was impressive range, the high reach of powerful Allied AA guns forced them to fly at the extremity of their performance, up to 9,000m (5½ miles) against well-defended land targets. Electrically heated suits were worn by crews who carried sufficient oxygen for about four hours, so consumption on longer flights had to be carefully monitored. High altitudes marginalized bombing accuracy. With a standard crew complement of seven, photo-reconnaissance mission Bettys carried an extra photographer, and command aircraft usually had an extra officer as observer, resulting in eight crew. Long-range reconnaissance missions sometimes carried two extra observers. The Betty's Achilles' heel was its lack of self-sealing petrol tanks. The crew of the land-attack corps did not wear parachutes, thus incurring higher crew losses than warranted.

While there were two land-based Betty units at Rabaul during Operation *Ro-Go*, there was consensus at command level that these should not be used for daytime attacks against shipping due to the punitive effectiveness of USN ship-borne AA. Instead, the Bettys would be used for small-scale night nuisance raids or torpedo attacks. The latter would be made individually or in small groups. The first Betty group based at Vunakanau at the time was 702 Ku under Captain Kuno Shuzo, a unit which had considerable night-flying expertise. The other group was 751 Ku, commanded by Captain Sata Naohiro, whose role was defined as patrol; however, the shortage of bomber inventory saw this unit also used for torpedo attacks.

The cockpit of a G3M2 Nell climbing out of Rabaul. The observer on the left behind the pilots often acted as an aircraft commander depending on his seniority.

Zero-sen

The backbone of Operation *Ro-Go* remained the infamous Zero-sen fighter. In addition to the redoubtable A6M2 operated by the carrier and land-based units, Rabaul's land-based fighter units also operated the A6M3 Model 22s and clipped-wing Model 32s. Later Model 22s were equipped with the Mk II long-barrel 20mm cannon, an improved and effective air-to-air weapon. The 204 Ku weapons testing center, located not far from Vunakanau, unsuccessfully trialled, *inter alia*, the use of 30mm aerial canon, but these were never installed.

The Zero-sen of 201 Ku comprised Model 22s and Model 21s. The unit's *hikotaicho* was Lieutenant Kawai Shiro, a veteran who had originally arrived in the New Guinea theater in January 1942, first as a *chutaicho* with Chitose Ku, then leading 4 Ku as *hikotaicho* until it was amalgamated into Tainan Ku in April 1942. However, by early October 1943, 201 Ku had become the sole defender of Buin. Just before the commencement of Operation *Ro-Go*, its nine surviving airworthy fighters at Buin were evacuated to Buka, with its entire ground echelon withdrawn to Rabaul by sea. Once it regathered at Rabaul, it was led by Lieutenant Oba Yoshio, the only operational officer still alive after months of intense combat. Following the cessation of Operation *Ro-Go*, 201 Ku was withdrawn to Saipan in early January 1944 when it became clear it lacked sufficient resources to sustain combat.

Alongside 201 Ku's Zero-sen at Lakunai was 204 Ku, the fighter unit which saw the most extended and heaviest combat of any Zero-sen unit in the South Seas theater. The severe attrition of Rabaul's fighter units in mid-1943 saw the depleted fighter wing of 582 Ku amalgamated with 204 Ku, then withdrawn to Rabaul just before the commencement of Operation *Ro-Go*. As such, the unit was by now operating a mixed bag of Model 21, 22, and 32 Zero-sen and was a key defender against the Allied November series of Rabaul raids. On January 26, 1944, its remaining dozen battle-worn Zero-sen were withdrawn to Truk.

A line-up for 204 Ku Model 21 and 22 Zero-sen at Buin with yellow fuselage bands, looking north. The unit's two *chutai* colors were red and yellow, but the unit operated with three *chutai* in late 1943, the third color unclear.

Over at Tobera, Lieutenant Commander Okamoto Harutoshi had become 253 Ku's *hikotaicho* on August 18, 1943. Following service in Bougainville in September 1943, the unit again returned to Tobera as the only fighter unit in the 25th Air Flotilla. Okamoto remained *hikotaicho* throughout Operation *Ro-Go*, serving 253 Ku until January 19, 1944. Stemming from Okamoto's defense of Rabaul during and after the operation, a patriotic war song lauding the unit's achievements was composed in Japan, titled "Souretsu! Okamoto Butai" (Hail the Heroic Okamoto Unit). By the end of January 1944, 253 Ku had become the only fighter unit able to credibly defend Rabaul, as the severe attrition rate had worn down all other fighter units.

Contrary to most Allied histories written about the 1943 period in the Pacific, the Zero-sen more than held its own in aerial combat, and in fact often scored more favorably than the American fighters with which it fought, including the F6F Hellcat. At the extreme of wrong claims is the one oft-cited that the Corsair scored against the Zero at a ratio of ten-to-one. A comparison of operational logs from both sides shows it closer to one-to-one. A clue to the Zero-sen's worth is taken from Operation *Ro-Go*'s November 8 battle with VMF-212 Corsairs of which the USMC pilots recorded, "Our pilots were impressed with the speed of the Zeke in particular. Zekes, even though well hit (one raked from spinner to fin) did not fire or explode."

The A6M5 Model 52 made a consistent appearance during Operation *Ro-Go*, and can be credited to recommendations made from the South Seas theater. In Japan around mid-1943 considerations were given as to how the Zero-sen's speed and armament could be improved. This resulted in the Model 52 with its shorter wingspan with rounded wingtips. The first Model 52 was delivered to Rabaul at the end of October 1943, only two months after this final model of the Zero had gone into production in August 1943. Mitsubishi made continual adjustments to the Model 52 airframe, including thicker wing skins, pilot protection, and armament changes to the cannon. All alterations incur compromise, and these modifications added considerable weight to the airframe, resulting in less maneuverability.

A 204 Ku Model 52 Zero-sen taxies at Lakunai in late 1943. These late models were ubiquitous at Rabaul from October 1943 onwards. A handful of Model 22s were retro-fitted with multiple-stack exhaust stub systems as seen here.

Meanwhile, in the South Seas front line, relentless attrition from combat and bombings placed fighter serviceability in jeopardy. Spares became scarce, and engineers through necessity often cannibalized parts from other airframes. Despite the introduction of the Model 22 and 52 series Zeros, the Model 21 remained ubiquitous throughout, although it was rarely, if ever, seen in the inventories of 253 Ku. The Model 21 also remained ever-present to carrier units which fought alongside Rabaul's land-based units during Operation *Ro-Go*.

Zero operations could extend to 30,000ft, sometimes higher, and combats which developed into widespread engagements required good communication. However, radios were notoriously ineffective in all model Zeros, exacerbated by hot tropical conditions and poor shielding and grounding. Restricted transmissions saw exasperated IJN engineers remove all radio equipment in some units, leaving Zero pilots to revert to the old way of hand signals for communication. Thus, a lack of command control plagued Zero-sen operations throughout Operation *Ro-Go*.

Judy

The Type 2 Carrier Reconnaissance D4Y1-C Judy was first assigned to the First Carrier Division in mid-1943 and played a key role in Operation *Ro-Go*, with Judys from *Zuikaku* and *Shokaku* operating as a combined detachment. At Rabaul the reconnaissance version was also operated by 151 Ku, while a dive-bomber version was operated by 501 Ku. All models had two fixed forward-firing 7.7mm machine guns; however, these were the early version of the D4Y1. 501 Ku had been activated on July 1, 1943, headed by Captain Sakata Yoshito, who also served as executive officer. Commander Kubo Kiyoshi served as *hikotaicho*, but by the time of Operation *Ro-Go* the unit struggled to keep half a dozen Judys airworthy, hence the welcome addition of the carrier-based contingent.

A D4Y1-C Judy reconnaissance aircraft preparing to depart Vunakanau in late 1943. The crewman to the far left carries an aerial camera for the mission. Note also the long-range tank attached underneath the starboard wing.

Val

The dive-bomber that populated Rabaul's land-based units and the carrier units during Operation *Ro-Go* was the Model 22 D3A2 Val. With a more powerful powerplant than its predecessor, the Model 11, it cruised about 20 knots faster, and had improved climb and high-altitude performance. Its defensive armament was limited to two fixed 7.7mm forward-firing machine guns and a single flexible 7.7mm on a swing mount operated by the observer in the rear cockpit. Although well suited to shipping attacks, it had to get low to deliver its ordnance, where it was easily picked off by high-performance Allied fighters and ship-borne AA. Land-based Vals routinely lugged a 250kg (550lb) centerline-slung bomb; however, for more distant missions, the Vals were impaired by the carriage of a hefty fuselage drop-tank.

DEFENDER'S CAPABILITIES

Operation *Ro-Go* was intended as a series of decisive air operations, to push Allied forces away from increasingly threatened Japanese strongholds. Since the operation unfolded at the same time the Allies were launching their own offensive, these forces had already put strong defensive strategies in place. Increasingly throughout the campaign, the role of attacker versus defender became blurred, whereby often the attacker became defender and vice versa. Admiral Koga's decision to move full attention to the Torokina landing resulted in effective defence by the Americans and invites the question of how they held so successfully and resolutely to the beachhead with minimal losses.

A J1N1-S of 151 Ku at Lakunai taken at low level during the November 2 Fifth Air Force strike.

Logistics and materiel

An underestimated factor in SOPAC operations was the overwhelming amount of reserve materiel and air power available to Allied forces during the campaign. In the event reserves were not required, however, all the forward-based air power and its supporting resources came courtesy of sophisticated US supply chains. These inevitably led back to the massive military complex built on the island of Espiritu Santo in the New Hebrides and, to a lesser degree, forward support bases at Guadalcanal and rearward ones at New Caledonia. The distance to Guadalcanal from the beachhead was 348 nautical miles, and Espiritu Santo a further 912. The challenges of these distances were lessened by the fact US forces had become well versed in how to manage supply chains along these routes. They had also developed multifarious resources to do so.

By the time of Operation *Ro-Go*, four major military airfields had been built on Espiritu Santo, supplemented by a USN seaplane overhaul base. The large island's Segond Channel offered tailor-made geography upon which had been built a comprehensive suite of naval docking and supply operations. Furthermore, Espiritu Santo lay outside the range of Japanese bombers, although several long-range reconnaissance missions had been made by H8K1 Emily flying boats earlier in 1943.

The size and importance of Espiritu Santo as a logistics base cannot be overstated. This view looks over Segond Channel toward Aore Island. The Quonset huts house, *inter alia*, headquarters, centers and facilities for service and overhaul squadrons, transport detachments, training, instrument overhauls meteorological facilities, and recreational and communications centers.

The first US military presence at Espiritu Santo appeared on April 23, 1942, from Efate via a J2F-5 Duck amphibian. Its passengers were part of the vanguard of "Task Force A" headed by Brigadier General William Rose, whose job was to survey the island for suitable airfield locations. From this inaugural visit a massive interwoven military complex had since grown. Rose chose a site just inland from Pallikulo Bay, and Bomber One, as it came to be known, was ready for operations only 13 days after first surveyed. Bomber Two, known also as Pekoa, had been opened on January 6, 1943. The USMC wanted its own airfield and completed one on November 18, 1942 on the northern tip of Turtle Bay on the island's eastern coast. MAG-11 began moving supplies into Turtle Bay almost immediately, and the field's role grew to incorporate aircrew rehabilitation, pilot training, staging and assembly platform areas for USMC aircraft, and, critically, an aircraft maintenance base. Santo's fourth airfield, called Bomber Three or Luganville, was completed on July 15, 1943.

Neither was there a shortage of forward airfields to provide land-based CAPs (Combat Air Patrols) for the Torokina beachhead and US shipping. All of these had been hard-won in a series of battles. Guadalcanal now boasted four major airfields and cantonments of supplies including ordnance, fuel, and oil. Around New Georgia were the forward airfields of Segi, Munda, Ondonga, and Barakoma. Fighter replenishments were easily ferried into these fields from Guadalcanal as needs be.

Strategy

An initial defender ruse was a distraction to the main Torokina landing initiated on October 28, when US forces occupied the northwest end of Choiseul as a feint. The limited operation diverted attention from the main Torokina landing, which commenced in the early hours of November 1. The Japanese suspected a major initiative was afoot when USN cruisers shelled the Buka area along with USN carrier aircraft, which conducted a series of strikes just after dawn on November 1. Other ships shelled the Shortland Islands, including AA positions, the floatplane bases at Poporang and Faisi Islands, and the airfield on Ballale Island.

Taken on November 26 at Torokina airfield, the SBD in the background was the first aircraft to land on the dirt runway the previous day.

The Allies ensured minimal resistance during the main landing when they deployed dozens of TBF Avengers and SBDs to strafe and bomb the Torokina beachhead before going ashore. Several SBDs then dropped smoke bombs to obfuscate visibility. A key defensive policy then came into play – despite unfavorable beach conditions, the unloading was carried out so swiftly that Japanese retaliatory attacks were mostly confined to moving ships.

Another key defensive tactic was the use of barrage balloons, which complicated access to the handful of Vals that managed to penetrate the US fighter CAPs. The USN balloons were a smaller size than the land-based type and were designated "Type ZKS Shipboard Barrage Balloon," manufactured by the Firestone Company. They were transported aboard LSTs (landing ships, tank) and had been first trialed aboard *LST 207* in Nouméa Harbor in the weeks leading up to the Torokina invasion. Several were initially deployed during the Mono Island operation in late October, and later eight LSTs each carried a balloon which arrived at the Torokina beachhead on November 4. They were easily handled aboard the LSTs and were close-hauled except when attacks were imminent.

Radar

The Allied defenders had to ward off numerous low-level Betty torpedo attacks, all of which were conducted at night. A key and highly successful weapon in deterring these was fire-control radar installed aboard capital USN warships. Their strength was that they worked well in any weather and any time, day or night. Ranging accuracy was excellent compared with the inherent inaccuracies of optical ranging; when operated properly, radar guidance ensured that opening salvos would bracket the incoming enemy aircraft rather than the less accurate optical method of "walking in" the rounds. Development of FD radar, used during Operation *Ro-Go*, had been first tested aboard destroyer USS *Roe* in September 1941. FD radar's main challenge had originally been elevation inaccuracy against low-flying torpedo planes, due to radar reflection from the ocean surface. To correct this, the sets had been upgraded in 1943 with a moving antenna, producing excellent low-level accuracy.

While the radar proved highly effective during Operation *Ro-Go*, and downed several torpedo-carrying Bettys, there were ongoing associated but different challenges, as outlined in a Task Force 39 (TF39) summary written late in the operation:

Wooden fins added to a Type 91 aerial torpedo so it can be stabilized in the slipstream underneath a Kate. When the torpedo struck the water at around 180 knots, the impact shattered the fins, leaving the steel fins to do the rest. The Type 91 was used by both Betty and Kate units throughout Operation *Ro-Go*.

Operations throughout the night of 10–11 November were uneventful except as noted in the Flag Plot Log. All ships remained at General Quarters stations from sunset until daylight . . . one enemy plane was shot down by USS *Spence* about 0154 . . . however our snooper shooting at night has been disappointing. Although most of our training has been in full radar control, our performance at night, even when shooting at comparatively slow float planes, has left a lot to be desired. The snoopers are as annoying and "sticky" as flies in the rainy season. They are persistent. They stay just out of range most of the time, and when they come in close their weaving tactics and changes of speed upset all gunnery solutions. At the first flash of a gun they dive for speed and make off using radical course changes. Sometimes they start in on bombing runs and if not fired on will follow through, releasing a bomb.

Sometimes floatplanes would simulate a torpedo attack, leading the radar operator to believe the attacker was a torpedo-carrying Betty. This meant that in the war zone, batteries were continually manned and alert throughout the night. The officer in Tactical Command had to continually monitor any plots. This meant that even uneventful nights were exhausting for the USN crews. Then, despite being denied the opportunity to sleep in the daytime due to aircraft attacks or threats, other mandatory duties nonetheless had to be carried out, such as cleaning gun batteries, replacing ammunition, or conducting routine maintenance. This was attended by the noise of repairing blast damage or other repairs. This meant that each successive night became more exhausting for USN sailors, leading to declining efficiency.

Air power

Constant CAPs patrolled both landing areas and shipping flotillas, including carriers. The refueling of 23 Munda-based VF-17 Corsairs aboard *Bunker Hill* was coordinated by the flight director aboard USS *Essex*. Prior to departing Munda, engineers had reattached the Corsairs' tail hooks, marking the first time in World War II that land-based aircraft had been refueled at sea before returning to duties. The use of ship-borne flight directors issuing coordinating radio instructions was a powerful tool in coordinating the movements of fighters, enabling efficient coverage of air space and directing them to enemy threats where identified. The IJN lacked similar capability.

CAMPAIGN OBJECTIVES

Given the eventual conduct and outcome of Operation *Ro-Go*, it is easy to overlook that the operation's primary focus at inception was to sever Allied supply routes in northeastern New Guinea, not the Solomons, bearing in mind that the Japanese viewed New Guinea and the Solomons as the same theater. This is precisely what Operation *Ro-Go*'s predecessor, Operation *I*, had done; three out of its four strikes were conducted against the New Guinea targets of Port Moresby, Milne Bay, and Oro Bay, with only one strike in the Solomons.

To understand the background to Operation *Ro-Go* and its change of focus, we need to consider the strategic view of New Guinea from mid-1943 onwards through Japanese eyes. After losing Lae and other strongholds along the northern New Guinea coast barely a month before, the main Japanese stronghold in New Guinea had defaulted to the Wewak area and its northern coastline, especially the air bases there. The Japanese Army Air Force (JAAF) 6th Flying Division, previously headquartered in Rabaul, was now based in that area, spread around Dagua, Awar, Hansa Bay, Alexishafen, and Madang. The importance of the JAAF's New Guinea campaign had seen the JAAF 7th Flying Division transferred to New Guinea in mid-1943, underlining the importance with which Imperial General Headquarters regarded the New Guinea theater. The joining of the 6th and 7th Flying Divisions had created the 4th Air Army, a powerful air force.

Although Japanese operations in the Burma campaign had ramped up, and large-scale operations had recommenced in China, the creation of the 4th Air Army saw nearly half of JAAF air strength ensconced in New Guinea by late 1943. All Japanese forces in New Guinea were forced to rely on the strength of the JAAF to guarantee shipping supplies, right down to basic food provisions. However, shipping was regularly being attacked and sunk in the face of growing Allied air power courtesy of the USAAF Fifth Air Force. As such, it was envisaged that a major "knockout" operation could halt these attacks. At this juncture, Koga had not ruled out targets in the Solomons; it was just that New Guinea targets would receive more attention. Koga had weighty considerations to mull over, no one doubted that.

VMSB-144 SBD-5 #119 about to make a morning run on the first day of the Torokina invasion of November 1. Note the smoke bomb slung underneath the fuselage. Paruata Island is offshore mid-photo while smoke from previous bombs dropped by TBFs is visible ashore.

OPPOSITE AIR POWER AT RABAUL, OPERATION *RO-GO*, NOVEMBER 1943

By late 1943 Henderson Field had grown into a massive logistics base, full of USMC, USN, and Thirteenth Air Force aircraft. It was a far cry from the half-finished field captured from the Japanese one and a half years previously. This view looks north toward Tulagi. The logistical buildup at this one Allied Solomons airfield alone was on par with Vunakanau.

At Truk, no specific New Guinea targets had so far been drawn up, as strike targets would be decided upon arrival at Rabaul in consultation with 11th Fleet air staff who knew the New Guinea theater best. However, even as air crews were being briefed at Truk on Operation *Ro-Go*'s broad principles, the landscape was changing rapidly. On October 27, New Zealand soldiers and troops from a US Seabee battalion occupied Mono Island with minimal Japanese resistance; the New Zealanders had just undertaken their first opposed amphibious operation since Gallipoli. The solitary Japanese platoon on Mono stopped communicating shortly after the invasion, causing consternation at Rabaul. It was possible that the Allied intent was to build yet another airfield on the road to Rabaul; nonetheless, at this juncture Koga still prevaricated. As yet, the development did not warrant a major shift of focus for Operation *Ro-Go*.

The Allied campaign to isolate Rabaul, Operation *Cartwheel*, was both ongoing and accelerating. Rather than assault the heavily defended complex, Allied command had determined the fortress would be isolated by capturing surrounding bases. Rabaul's protection from the advance up the Solomons was the massive island of Bougainville. Japanese association with Bougainville had commenced back on January 23, 1942, when Buka had been raided by floatplanes from cruiser *Tone* during the invasion of Rabaul. The only casualty of this strike was Australian launch *Nugget*, carrying government records, cash, and a telegraph radio. Meanwhile, down at Kieta on Bougainville's east coast, Mavis flying boats had circled the town on January 16 and 20, one of which landed on the harbor, taxied around awhile, then departed with no further action. The Japanese had then occupied the

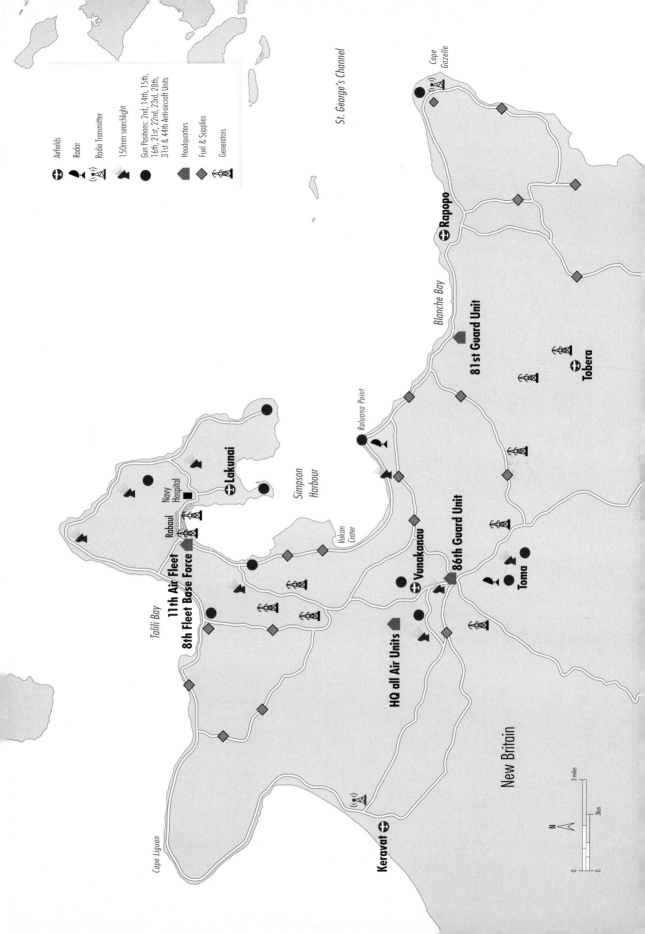

St. George's Channel

Cape
Gazelle

Rapopo

Blanche Bay

81st Guard Unit

Tobera

Raluana Point

86th Guard Unit

Vunakanau

Toma

HQ all Air Units

New Britain

Keravat

Cape Liguan

Talili Bay

11th Air Fleet
8th Fleet Base Force

Rabaul

Navy Hospital

Lakunai

Simpson Harbour

Vulcan Crater

N

3 miles

3km

Airfields

Radar

Radio Transmitter

150mm searchlight

Gun Positions: 2nd, 14th, 15th, 16th, 21st, 22nd, 23rd, 28th, 31st & 44th Anti-aircraft Units

Headquarters

Fuel & Supplies

Generators

RNZAF P-40 pilots in the Solomons. New Zealand P-40s regularly patrolled the beachhead, USN shipping, and carriers throughout Operation *Ro-Go*.

island back in March 1942, with modest forces which overwhelmed the scattered Australian contingents. However, from these curious and restrained beginnings, by late 1943 Japanese forces in Bougainville had grown into a juggernaut.

Following the Allied occupation of Mono Island, on the very next day, October 28, US forces occupied the northwest end of Choiseul, comprising a restrained maneuver designed to divert attention from the main game: a full-scale landing at Cape Torokina, Bougainville, planned for the early hours of November 1. This feint prompted Rabaul to divert a squadron of warships toward Choiseul. These ships, along with Bettys from Vunakanau, failed to find substantive Allied shipping in the area. With no evidence that either Allied operation was a major one, Koga authorized Operation *Ro-Go* to proceed, with focus to remain on New Guinea. Then, as the carrier aircraft assigned to the operation winged their way to Truk on November 1, the Allies commenced their Torokina landing, an initiative which directly threatened Rabaul.

The primary objectives of Operation *Ro-Go*, designed as offensive strikes against New Guinea targets, were turned on their head. Instead, Koga reprioritised the operation to laser-focus on the protection of Rabaul. Thus, the incumbents found themselves flying a series of defensive and offensive missions against Allied air power, shipping, and land targets centered around Rabaul, Torokina, the Treasury Islands, and Empress August Bay. Not one Operation *Ro-Go* mission was flown against New Guinea.

THE CAMPAIGN

The main challenge of the first day of Operation *Ro-Go* on November 1 was marked by the requirement to safely ferry 173 aircraft from Truk down to Rabaul. The flight took the aircraft due south for a distance over open water of exactly 700 nautical miles. The three main differing aircraft types with different performances saw them divided into three groups, leaving at slightly staggered times. Diversions en route were not available, as there was nowhere else to land. This meant an early morning departure to avoid weather buildup, and pathfinder navigation aircraft to assist in both leading the formations and providing the relevant forecasts. The uneventful ferry flight was a feat in itself and reflects well on the training of IJN crews for long-distance navigation.

Division officers Lt Notomi Kenjiro led *Zuikaku*'s complement of 27 Zero-sen, Lt Sato Tomeo led 19 from *Zuiho*, and Lt Sakami Ikuro headed three dozen from *Shokaku*, a total of 82 fighters. The high complements of fighters from *Zuikaku* and *Shokaku* reflect reinforcements provided to the carriers at Truk which had not been placed aboard ship, and allocated to fresh pilots. After a pre-dawn departure, the Zero-sen arrived at Rabaul at 1050hrs after a delivery flight of nearly five hours, followed by 40 Kates and 45 Vals. The aircraft dispersed themselves between Tobera, Lakunai, and Vunakanau airfields. Six D4Y1-C Judy reconnaissance aircraft from the three carriers also settled into Vunakanau. They would operate as one detachment, providing key observation reports in forthcoming days, led by *Shokaku*'s Lt Kimura Satoshi who headed the combined unit.

The aircrew who clambered from their aircraft at Rabaul included engineers who had flown as passengers in several Vals and Kates, all of whom would be housed in extra tents set up around the airfields. Extra room had been found for officers in wooden barracks. However, when they arrived they were in for unexpected news.

While they had been sleeping the night before, and during the ferry flight from Truk, US air and naval power had appeared from nowhere and invaded Bougainville at Torokina, code-named Operation *Cherry Blossom* by its instigators. Rabaul's staff officers pored over maps, examining options. It was only a few days ago that Commander of the Combined

VF-17 Corsair 17656 Squadron #5 at Torokina in January 1944, assigned to Lt Thomas Killifer, one of the pilots who refueled aboard USS *Bunker Hill* on November 11.

Table 1: Operational structure of Base 11th Air Fleet air units, November 1, 1943

Commander Vice Admiral Kusaka Jinichi

FORCE	UNIT	TYPE	LOCATION	ROLE
5th Attack Force (Headquarters at Rabaul)	251 Kokutai (Cdr Kusumoto Ikuto)	J1N1-S Irving	Lakunai	Night fighter and reconnaissance
	253 Kokutai (Cdr Fukuda Taro)	Model 21, 22, 32, and 52 Zero	Tobera	Fighter
	702 Kokutai (Captain Kuno Shuzo)	G4M1 Betty	Vunakanau	Bomber
	751 Kokutai (Captain Sata Naohiro)	G4M1 Betty	Vunakanau	Bomber – patrol
6th Attack Force (Headquarters recently returned to Rabaul from Buin)	201 Kokutai (Cdr Nakano Chujiro)	Model 21 and 22 Zero	Lakunai	Fighter – cover
	204 Kokutai (Cdr Shibata Takeo)	Model 21, 22, and 32 Zero	Lakunai	Fighter
	501 Kokutai (Captain Sakata Yoshito)	D4Y Judy	Vunakanau	Dive-bomber
	582 Kokutai (Captain Minematsu Iwao)	D3A2 Val	Vunakanau Buka	Dive-bomber
Reconnaissance	151 Kokutai (Vacant)	J1N1-S Irving D4Y Judy	Lakunai	Reconnaissance
Sea Base Force	938 Kokutai (Cdr Terai Kunizo)	F1M2 Pete E13A1 Jake	Rabaul, Buka, and Shortlands	Night recce/attack/anti-submarine
	958 Kokutai (Captain I'ida Rinjuro)	F1M2 Pete E13A1 Jake	Rabaul, Buka, Kavieng, and Shortlands	Night recce/attack/anti-submarine

Table 2: First Carrier Division air units in Rabaul, November 1, 1943

Commander Vice Admiral Ozawa Jisaburo

CARRIER	TYPE	LOCATION	ROLE
Zuikaku	Model 21 Zero D3A2 Val B5N2 Kate	Tobera, Lakunai, and Vunakanau	Attack
Shokaku	Model 21 Zero D3A2 Val B5N2 Kate	Lakunai and Vunakanau	Attack
Zuiho	Model 21 Zero B5N2 Kate	Lakunai and Vunakanau	Attack
(Combined detachment *Zuiho*, *Shokaku*, and *Zuikaku*)	D4YC Judy	Vunakanau	Reconnaissance

Fleet, Admiral Koga Mineichi, had reverted Operation *Ro-Go*'s objective back from the Solomons theater to New Guinea instead. There had been prevarication leading up to the launch of the operation, and for good reasons. On October 27, New Zealand soldiers and troops from the Navy Construction Battalion (Seabees) had landed on Mono Island, with the intention of building yet another airfield closer to Rabaul. Curiously, the New Zealanders had just undertaken their first opposed amphibious operation since Gallipoli. The solitary Japanese platoon on Mono stopped communicating shortly after the invasion, causing consternation at Rabaul.

Anticipating trouble, and as a precautionary move, commander of the 11th Air Fleet at Rabaul, Vice Admiral Kusaka Jinichi,

Explosions can be seen during the attack by USS *Saratoga* aircraft against the Japanese airfields which lay on both sides of Buka passage on November 1, 1943. Buka airfield is on the right, with Bonis to the left.

had recalled a contingent of 582 Ku D3A2 Val dive-bombers back to Vunakanau from Kavieng, leaving the major portion of these dive-bombers at Buka. Then, the following day, October 28, US forces launched an occupation on the northwest end of Choiseul. The purpose of this modest operation was to serve as a diversion from a planned major landing at Cape Torokina, on Bougainville, planned for the early hours of November 1. Throughout the week of the Choiseul invasion, US Marines undertook a series of hit-and-run raids over a wide area guided by islanders. The diversion worked exactly as planned, for Rabaul headed a squadron of destroyers in the direction of Choiseul led by light cruiser *Nagara*. Six 702 Ku Bettys from Vunakanau reconnoitered and bombed Munda at night, expecting to find substantive Allied shipping but had trouble finding the target in the weather. A curiosity from this raid is that Flying Chief Petty Officer Yoshimoto Yoshiaki's Betty was shot down in the early hours of November 1 by a VMF-75(N) night-fighter F4U Corsair, guided by the radar station on Vella Lavella. Yoshimoto is listed in the relevant Japanese operations log as "lost to weather," while two of his comrades diverted to bomb Barakoma on the way home.

With no enemy shipping in sight around the Bougainville area, Koga authorized Operation *Ro-Go* to proceed with New Guinea targets, to be decided after consultation with 11th Fleet staff officers who had experience in the field. The Japanese suspected they had been duped when USN cruisers shelled Buka airfield and nearby complexes followed by air strikes from USN aircraft from carriers USS *Saratoga* and *Princeton*. These made four strikes just after dawn on November 1, coincidentally at the same time the Japanese carrier planes were leaving Truk for the ferry flight down to Rabaul.

Radio calls from Buka informing Rabaul of their dilemma were supplemented by more radio transmissions from the Shortland Islands revealing that they too were under bombardment. The culprit in this case was light cruiser USS *Montpelier*, using its 5-inch batteries to strike AA positions on Morgusaia Island, the floatplane bases at Poporang and Faisi Islands, and finally the airfield on Ballale Island. However, all these strikes served as a distraction to the main game – the invasion of Torokina. At 0700hrs on November 1, 31 TBF Avengers dropped bombs, including seven 1-tonners, and seven SBDs strafed the beachhead and dropped smoke bombs. These attacks prepared the way for the landing force based around the US 3rd Marine Division anchored in Empress Augusta Bay, just offshore Torokina. Situated well away from any of Hyakutake's main forces, and against the backdrop of Mt Bagana, an active volcano of 6,086ft, the landing was met with sporadic gunfire, including machine-gun fire from Paruata Island.

OPPOSITE BOUGAINVILLE AREA SHOWING THE ALLIED APPROACH TO CAPE TOROKINA

Carrier strikes against the Japanese airfield at Buka pre-empted the Torokina landing. This had little impact on Japanese air power as nearly all of it emanated from Rabaul. There were few Japanese troops to oppose the landing, however forces were later moved to surround the beachhead. Commodore Lawrence Reifsnider commanded the landing forces.

By the end of this first day, Operation *Cherry Blossom* had established a modest perimeter, and the first wave of merchantmen had unloaded stores at their assigned beachheads. Rabaul dispatched a reasonably substantial Japanese naval force to disrupt the landing which, overnight on November 1–2, unsuccessfully clashed with USN cruisers and destroyers during the Battle of Empress Augusta Bay. The American task force was still withdrawing their merchantmen from the beachhead when US reconnaissance aircraft detected the approaching Japanese fleet. USN ships which had shelled Buka and the Shortlands quickly reestablished themselves to block the entrance to Empress Augusta Bay. The Japanese approached from the northwest; however, in the early hours of November 2 cruiser *Haguro* was struck amidships by an American aerial attack, necessitating slowing the entire flotilla in order to protect it against further attack. The Japanese ships subsequently became separated in the confusion of night combat and sustained heavy losses, resulting in their return to Rabaul.

Meanwhile, on the second day of the invasion, the remaining stores and equipment were unloaded from the transports. This operation proceeded smoothly, with each ship reverting to its own unique assigned area. The unloading crews had practised near Havannah Harbor on Efate several weeks prior and had the technique down to a fine art. Over the course of the next few days, the US troops ashore consolidated their beachhead and secured the perimeter – firmly established by the closing hours of November 3.

Defending Torokina

The Torokina beachhead, the ships guarding it, and the air power in the vicinity now defaulted to Operation *Ro-Go*'s primary objective. It might be argued, in essence, that

LST 398 unloads on the northeast coast of Purata Island on the morning of November 1 shortly after it beached there at 0835hrs. Landing vessels like this became a prime target for the few Vals which made it past Allied fighters.

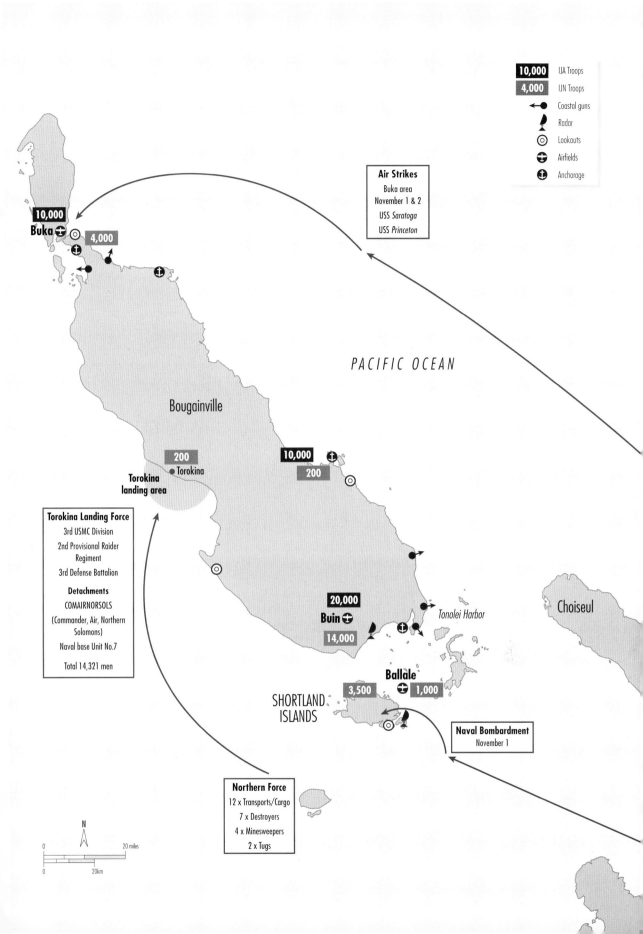

10,000 IJA Troops

4,000 IJN Troops

Coastal guns

Radar

Lookouts

Airfields

Anchorage

Air Strikes
Buka area
November 1 & 2
USS *Saratoga*
USS *Princeton*

10,000
Buka

4,000

PACIFIC OCEAN

Bougainville

200
• Torokina

**Torokina
landing area**

10,000
200

Torokina Landing Force
3rd USMC Division
2nd Provisional Raider
Regiment
3rd Defense Battalion

Detachments
COMAIRNORSOLS
(Commander, Air, Northern
Solomons)
Naval base Unit No.7

Total 14,321 men

Choiseul

20,000
Buin
14,000

Tonolei Harbor

Ballale
3,500   **1,000**

**SHORTLAND
ISLANDS**

Naval Bombardment
November 1

Northern Force
12 x Transports/Cargo
7 x Destroyers
4 x Minesweepers
2 x Tugs

N

0 ——— 20 miles

0 ——— 20km

OPPOSITE TOROKINA LANDING

The signal to prepare for the November 1 landing at Torokina was given at 0645hrs and shore bombardment was ceased at 0721hrs, shortly after which the US troops went ashore. The landing was complicated by a narrow beach which harbored rough surf.

Operation *Ro-Go* had reverted to a defensive campaign. While the carrier air contingent was en route from Truk, at Rabaul Admiral Kusaka authorized his base air force to conduct the first strike of Operation *Ro-Go* against the US ships offshore Torokina. American air power was key to defending the invasion as the ships sailed for the beachhead and included night-fighters. These were provided by three Marine PV-1 Venturas from Barakoma assigned to VMF-531(N), which commenced patrolling in the late evening of October 31. A rotation system of 32 fighters was scheduled to patrol overhead during daylight hours, selected from USAAF 339th Fighter Squadron P-38 Lightnings, Marine Corsairs, and RNZAF P-40Ms. These were land-based at airfields around New Georgia in the central Solomons.

Such Allied protection, even without intervention from the Japanese, would prove costly. The first loss occurred at 0455hrs at Barakoma when a VMF-212 Corsair crashed into a returning Ventura night-fighter, killing Corsair pilot 1/Lt George Grill. Ground crews clearing the runway were disrupted at 0505hrs when a lone Betty dropped six 60kg (132lb) bombs near the airfield. This was one of a pair of 702 Ku Bettys from Vunakanau which had diverted to Barakoma in the poor weather, flown by Flying Petty Officer 2nd Class O'otaki Isuro. When the US fighter departure sequence continued, a VMF-211 Corsair lost power on takeoff and ditched offshore, this time at Ondonga, although its pilot, 1/Lt Edwin McCaleb, was rescued. This was followed by another similar loss offshore Barakoma – this time a VMF-215 Corsair flown by 2/Lt Robert Keister.

Meanwhile, back at Vunakanau a 702 Ku Betty with a full complement of seven crew departed at 0830hrs to search sector N3 for US shipping. It had just reached top of climb at 25,000ft some 30 miles east of Cape St. George when a patrol of eight 339th Fighter Squadron P-38s led by Captain V. Harter dived through it and shot it down. Such was the surprise that radio operator Flyer1c Miyawaki Harunobu had no chance to get away even a cursory radio call. When Vunakanau's central communications center never heard from it again, it logged the reasons for the bomber's disappearance as "unclear."

Under the pressing circumstances of formidable Allied activity, Rabaul ordered the redeployment of its key reconnaissance assets stationed in the Shortland Islands up to Buka. The main resources to be transferred were 938 Ku E13A1 Jake reconnaissance floatplanes, and on the morning of November 1 the unit commander, IJN Commander Terai Kunizo, tasked pilot Lt (jg) Nishiyama Terukazu to lead a detachment of the Jakes to Buka, where they would primarily be used for night-time reconnaissance and attack missions. Nishiyama organized two pairs of Jakes to conduct the detachment's first recce from Buka the following evening, November 2, departing Buka at 1910hrs and 2100hrs.

This portrait of two VF-17 Corsair pilots showcases USN flight gear of the times, including parachute harness and survival knife.

The other primary floatplane unit in the South Seas theater was 958 Ku. It already had detachments stationed at Buka, Rabaul, and Kavieng, but focused its operations on anti-submarine patrols. Unit commander Captain I'ida Rinjuro also dispatched a contingent to Buka in the same timeframe, falling under 938 Ku's command structure there. For the Allies, these pesky floatplanes were a nuisance throughout Operation *Ro-Go*; they appeared all over the place, often dropping two 60kg (132lb) bombs from low altitude. In the face of poor weather, they made a focused effort to keep Rabaul updated with USN shipping positions, movements, and sizes.

First strike – November 1

The first Japanese air attack incorporated an oddity. The first dedicated D4Y Judy dive-bomber unit to have seen action in the South Seas theater was 501 Ku, its advance echelon having arrived at Rabaul the previous month. During Operation *Ro-Go*, its Judys dropped air-to-air phosphorus bombs into enemy formations, often being misidentified as Ki-61 Tonys. This first strike would see one 501 Ku Judy accompany the Vals.

Japanese shells explode on the water offshore Torokina during the initial invasion on November 1. Shortly after this photo was taken, several 582 Vals bombed the beachhead but incurred little damage.

Zero pilot Lt (jg) Fukuda Sumio from 204 Ku was tasked to coordinate the first strike. His aircraft commenced departing Rabaul at 0620hrs. Radar aboard destroyer USS *Conway* warned of the approaching Japanese, and the destroyer's flight director vectored the Allied fighter CAP toward the three groups of incoming enemy aircraft. These were broken down into 24 Zero-sen from 201 Ku and 20 from 204 Ku, attending the dive-bomber contingent comprising eight 582 Ku Vals accompanied by the solitary 501 Ku Judy.

These groups were separately engaged by 16 339th Fighter Squadron P-38s led by Lt-Col John McGinn of 347th Fighter Group HQ, eight USAAF P-40s, and eight more from RNZAF 18 Squadron based at Ondonga. These Allied fighters claimed a total of 16 Japanese aircraft. During the melee several Vals broke through to attack the transports anchored offshore and, despite emergency turns by several ships, managed a near-miss on destroyer USS *Wadsworth* which killed two sailors. The ships' AA gunners claimed a further four Zero-sen as they strafed the beachhead. These American claims, in fact, were reasonable against the substantial losses incurred from the raid. When the Japanese returned to Rabaul's airfields from 0920hrs onwards, the true cost soon became apparent; eight 201 Ku Zero-sen were missing and two more had ditched, their pilots rescued. Another two were junked at Rabaul due to severe airframe damage. Three 204 Ku Zero-sen had been shot down, with one more written off at Rabaul. Three of the 582 Ku Vals had been shot down too, marking a total of 16 aircraft lost during combat. This is one of the rare occasions when the combined Allied claim of 20 aircraft closely matched the reality of Japanese losses; most Allied combat claims in the Pacific 1943 timeframe overclaim by a factor of between three to four.

A curious loss stemming from this combat occurred to RNZAF Flight Officer Ken Lumsden, flying NZ3068, one of the 18 Squadron P-40Ms. He was being pursued by two Zero-sen over the Torokina landing area, when his fighter was holed from AA fire from a USN destroyer. To make matters much worse, he was then attacked by a Corsair, forcing him to ditch. Rescued by an American barge, and after nearly being machine-gunned by the crew, who mistook his RNZAF red and white rescue flag as a Japanese one, Lumsden was finally safe. This incident, combined with similar and earlier ones experienced by P-40 Kittyhawks from RNZAF 14 and 15 Squadrons in mid-1943, convinced the RNZAF to change their roundel insignia to resemble USAAF ones. This was done by adding horizontal white bars to each side of the blue and white roundels.

Second strike – November 1

Following the dive-bombing attacks made by the Vals, the US merchantmen received warning at 1300hrs to repel another air attack. This followed a radar painting of around 100 incoming bogies, two of which the Allied CAP was vectored toward. Again, several Vals broke through but scored no hits, the nearest bombs exploding near transport USS *Legion*. As a follow-up, the beach was subjected to sporadic bombing and strafing which did little damage. By 1500hrs all the armed transports had returned to their designated unloading areas, where they resumed discharging; however, the attack had delayed the complete unloading of four. The entire task group left for Guadalcanal, but at

VF-17 Corsair Squadron #34 assigned to Lt (jg) Doris Freeman which he named "LA CITY LIMITS." Freeman appears at Torokina in February 1944, three months after the invasion.

2300hrs these four, still crammed with essential materiel, left the flotilla to return to the beachhead, where they completed unloading shortly after dawn on November 2.

This second attack closely resembled the first, involving an 1130hrs departure from Rabaul with a total of 42 Zero-sen: a dozen from 201 Ku, 16 from 204 Ku, joined by 14 from 253 Ku. Six 582 Ku Vals were accompanied again by a solitary 501 Ku Judy. The degree to which the 11th Air Fleet was lacking experienced leaders is reflected in the fact that a 253 Ku junior grade lieutenant, Umasawa Kanekichi, was assigned to lead the entire attack.

This was a frustrating day for a patrol of eight VMF-221 Corsairs which never made the fight due to a confused radio call that sent them off on the wrong vector. At 1330hrs eight VF-17 Corsairs swept the beachhead, where they intercepted nine Zero-sen making strafing passes and six Vals bombing the ships offshore. Led by Lt-Cdr Roger Hedrick, these Corsairs engaged a *chutai* of 253 Ku but claimed only one Zero-sen. Although they claimed no Vals, four were claimed by the ship's gunners. In fact, although not as costly as the first strike, two 582 Ku Vals were shot down by the ships, with two more lightly damaged. At 1345hrs eight VMF-215 Corsairs engaged around 20 Zero-sen, claiming three; Corsair pilot 1/Lt Robert Hanson went MIA during the fight. The retreating combined Zero-sen formation was pursued by an agitated VMF-215 which claimed three more Zero-sen. Most of the Japanese attackers had landed safely back at Rabaul by 1530hrs, with actual losses confined to four 253 Ku Zero-sen to fighters, and two Vals to ships' AA fire.

Two night strikes – November 1

With such a dire situation on their hands, the Japanese decided to launch two night attacks with dive-bombers. The first would strike the destroyers, which they correctly assessed would loiter offshore the Torokina beachhead, while a second Val strike would search for USN ships which the Japanese calculated would lurk to the east of Buka. Fighters were not assigned for night-time operations, so the Vals would operate by themselves.

For both strikes two Vals would each carry flares to illuminate targets. The first strike of six Vals departed Vunakanau at 1950hrs and headed due southeast for the 203-nautical-mile journey to Torokina, which in ideal conditions would take just over an hour and a half. However, the evening was marked by unsettled and persistent conditions, including squalls and thunderstorms. One Val turned back with mechanical troubles, and then four more became lost in the weather but eventually found their way home. One of the pathfinder Vals, with an extra crewmember aboard, disappeared in the murk.

Ground crew at Vunakanau grapple a 250kg bomb. These were slung underneath D3A2 Vals for shipping strikes.

Meanwhile, down at Buka, 582 Ku *chutaicho* Lt (jg) Suma Osamu was planning a later strike against USN ships. Suma was observer in the first Val to launch from Buka at 2300hrs; however, they soon struck the same capricious weather experienced by the previous aviators. The result was disastrous; one returned early with mechanical problems, while Suma's remaining eight Vals became separated. Only five returned to Buka, the other three swallowed in the weather.

The carrier forces strike – November 2

Late into the evening of November 1, Rabaul staff officers pored over the damage reports submitted by the returned Val aircrews. Unrestrained claims of USN ships sunk were farfetched, resulting from a combination of inexperience and wishful thinking. Regardless, even if half the claims made were imaginary, USN forces at the landing still posed a solid threat to Rabaul in both the short and longer terms.

Meanwhile, around Rabaul's airfields the carrier air contingent that had arrived the previous day saw ground crews busy themselves with fitting ordnance racks and other measures. These aircraft had to adjust their modus operandi, as operating from their ship, with its established facilities, was more efficient than some of the ad hoc systems they had to implement at short notice. It was important that the first carrier strike was successful, for it would showcase the ability of the carrier aviators, including the far-reaching distances of the D4Y1-C Judy reconnaissance detachment. *Shokaku's* Lt Kimura Satoshi conferred with *Zuikaku* officer Lt Baba Sakuhiko on how best to conduct the first reconnaissance mission of the day. The mission was critical, for the strike force would be relying heavily on Baba's report. It was decided his Judy's track would extend out to 200 nautical miles if necessary on a bearing of 138 degrees from Rabaul.

Baba departed at 0600hrs, seated as observer, and only 50 minutes later reported finding a flotilla 100 miles from Rabaul centered around four major ships. Ten minutes later, he sighted another group of ships 130 miles distant, these being the second flotilla of Rear Admiral Merrill's TF39 retiring from surface engagements of the previous night.

Back at Tobera, a raring Lt Notomi Kenjiro prepared to lead the inaugural carrier strike. Notomi had been chosen for many reasons, not the least of which was that he was an IJN legend, stemming from a disproportionate share of South Seas misadventure to date, all of which were well known throughout the fleet. Previously a division officer aboard *Akagi*, he had been later transferred to *Shoho*. After *Shoho* was sunk on May 7, 1942 during the Battle of the Coral Sea, Notomi had been forced to ditch offshore Deboyne Island, along with two others; Notomi's injuries were confined to a cut scalp. He returned to Rabaul aboard sea tender *Kiyokawa Maru*. Subsequently transferred to carrier *Shoho*, Notomi was again forced to ditch when the carrier was sunk on August 24, 1942 during the Battle of the Eastern

A 582 Ku D3A2 Val undergoes a wheel change at Vunakanau, sheltered by trees. Special maintenance detachments worked on these airframes distant from the main revetments and runways.

Solomons. This time rescued by a destroyer, Notomi had then been appointed as leader of *Zuikaku*'s air group, the position he now held.

Vals would be used to strike the US ships, with no Kates involved. Notomi authorized the strike force to leave Rabaul even before Baba's first report from his Judy pin-pointed its location, on the basis that the force was assuredly in the vicinity of Torokina. However, there was a major deficiency – the carrier-based Vals lacked ordnance racks to carry 250kg (550lb) bombs, and larger ones would have to be fitted. In the interim, and for this mission, each would carry only two 60kg (132lb) bombs, ineffective for the purpose of attacking ships as had been proven back in April during Operation *I*. The attack force comprised 18 Vals, nine each from *Zuikaku* and *Shokaku*.

Notomi organized his Zero-sen into four-fighter *shotai*, with the exception of the lead *Zuikaku shotai* which portended five, including Notomi. The full complement of 65 Zero-sen was created from two dozen from *Shokaku*, 25 from *Zuikaku*, and 16 from *Zuiho*. The slower Vals launched first at 0635hrs and set climb for 16,500ft, shepherded by the *Zuikaku* and *Shokaku* Zero-sen. The *Zuiho* Zero-sen, broken into defensive and attack formations, flew ahead of this main formation, varying their altitude from 13,000 to 20,000ft, and seeking trouble. On this first mission, engagement with Allied fighters would undoubtedly occur, the only questions being where and when.

The Allies were indeed anticipating a strong Japanese response and had launched their 32-fighter CAP in stages early that morning. Aboard the American ships and around the beachhead no one doubted Rabaul would send an air attack. The sky was clear, and excellent visibility prevailed over a calm sea. Decks were cleared and ammunition replenished. Of immediate concern was the destroyer USS *Foote*, crippled during the previous night's sea battle, which had fallen to the rear of the rest of the task force escorted by two more destroyers.

Meanwhile, over at Barakoma, the first fighter departures had again been interrupted by another brief bombing attack at 0455hrs by a 702 Ku Betty. First away was a division of four VMF-221 Corsairs at 0515hrs. The fighter director coordinating Allied air defense this time was aboard USS *Conway*, a Fletcher-class destroyer equipped with radar for such purpose. At 0710hrs eight VMF-212 Corsairs departed Barakoma as part of the CAP, but due to communications difficulties found no enemy fighters the entire day. One of these pilots,

OPPOSITE NOVEMBER 2, 1943, EARLY MORNING JAPANESE ATTACK AGAINST THE TOROKINA BEACHHEAD

VF-33 Hellcat #6 which participated in CAP duties during Operation *Ro-Go*, but seen here after it taxied into a ditch on December 10, 1943 at Barakoma.

1/Lt Thaddeus Trojnar, had quite the adventure when his engine quit at 33,000ft, the result of a frozen ignition system. It did not restart until he had descended to 15,000ft on glide, after which he returned to Barakoma.

At 0718hrs radar painted three groups of bogies at 50 miles' distance, and Torokina was warned by radio to prepare for attack. Then, at 0743hrs "General Quarters" was sounded among all USN ships in the vicinity. Around 0801hrs the ships' AA positions began tracking the incoming Japanese. The enemy formation flew directly over the incapacitated USS *Foote* and its escorts, but surprisingly ignored it as they could see bigger game on the horizon. They headed directly for the collective of cruisers and destroyers, which commenced to maneuver sharply to avoid the Vals' bombs, a tactic later much endorsed in the subsequent contact report as "turn, turn and turn again at high speed." These violent maneuvers produced their own challenges as the rapid change of relative bearings made it difficult for fire directors to keep gun sights on the enemy. Many of the lighter 20mm and 40mm guns fired prematurely, well out of range; however, the resultant bursting shells had the positive effect of dissuading several attackers.

The recipients of the Val attacks were primarily the cruisers and destroyers of TF39, namely *Montpelier*, *Cleveland*, *Denver*, *Columbia*, *Dyson*, *Spence*, *Converse*, and *Stanley*. The majority of Val attacks were made between 0805hrs and 0814hrs. During these attacks, conducted in three-aircraft *shotai*, one Val had its tail blown off by ships' AA, and another tried vainly to fly into flagship *Montpelier*'s bridge after being hit. Several more Vals were seen to crash into the bay and several parachutes were also reported. Some dove directly into the sea without pulling out, an indicator the pilot had been hit. The impression aboard the USN ships was that the attacking aviators were poor quality, and some were dissuaded even by automatic weapons

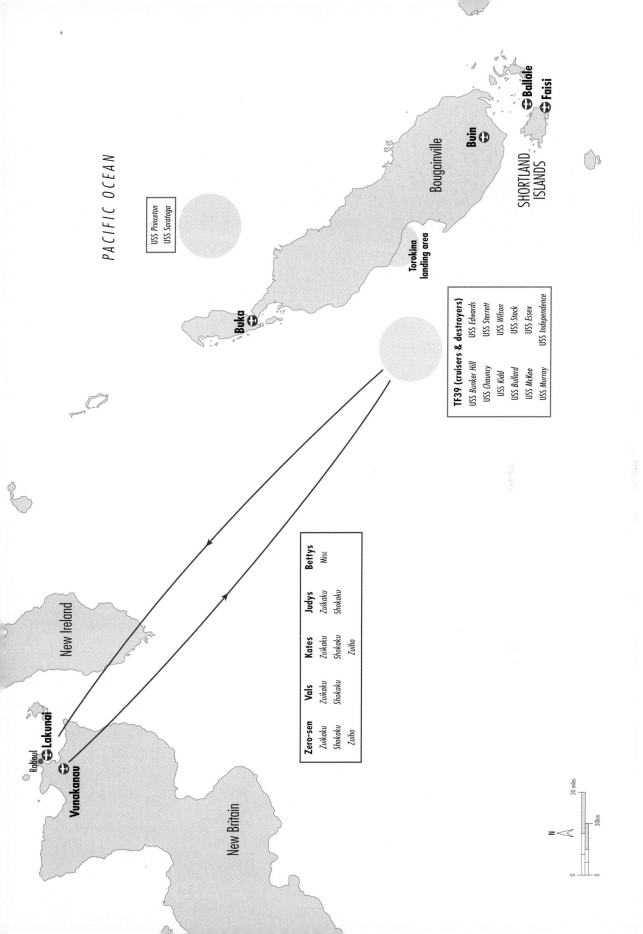

PACIFIC OCEAN

USS *Princeton*
USS *Saratoga*

Buka

Bougainville

Torokina
landing area

SHORTLAND
ISLANDS

Buin

Ballale
Faisi

TF39 (cruisers & destroyers)

USS *Bunker Hill*	USS *Edwards*
USS *Chauncy*	USS *Sterett*
USS *Kidd*	USS *Wilson*
USS *Bullard*	USS *Stack*
USS *McKee*	USS *Essex*
USS *Murray*	USS *Independence*

New Ireland

Rabaul
Lakunai
Vunakanau

New Britain

Zero-sen	**Vals**	**Kates**	**Judys**	**Bettys**
Zuikaku	*Zuikaku*	*Zuikaku*	*Zuikaku*	*Misc*
Shokaku	*Shokaku*	*Shokaku*	*Shokaku*	
Zuiho		*Zuiho*		

N

0   30 miles

0   30km

Zero-sen pilots at Lakunai being briefed around the time of Operation *Ro-Go*. Note the lieutenant in the background is distinguished by a lighter flight suit.

fire. In the confusion, the ships' gunners claimed to have downed a total of 20 Vals: *Montpelier* seven, *Denver* two, *Cleveland* seven, and *Columbia* four, more a reflection of the chaos at hand. In fact, six were shot down, each with a crew of two; the four *Zuikaku* Vals were flown by pilots FPO1c Shimokawa Haruo, FPO1c Inada Uemi, FPO1c Yamaki Tsutomu, and WO Tanaka Kichiki, and the two from *Shokaku* by pilots FPO1c Izuchi Natsuo and FPO1c Koizumi Shirou.

The Zero-sen, which had held off during the Val dive-bombing attacks to avoid AA fire, now proceeded to strafe the beaches, also making several close passes against ships anchored just offshore. After this the CAP fighters chased and fought the Japanese formations as they withdrew toward Rabaul. In the confusion there were two Allied units that failed to contact the enemy – eight VMF-215 Corsairs and four VF-17 Corsairs, which, after patrolling the beachhead area earlier, took the opportunity to strafe targets on the Shortland Islands instead. At 0800hrs eight RNZAF P-40Ms intercepted an estimated 30 Zero-sen, joined ten minutes later by eight 339th Fighter Squadron P-38s and VMF-221 Corsairs. At 0940hrs the Vals and Zero-sen commenced landing at Rabaul. Despite numerous claims of Zero-sen shot down across the Allied units, not one had been lost.

The Fifth Air Force strikes – November 2

After returning to their Rabaul airfields at mid-morning, the carrier crews recuperated. Many were rostered to participate in a follow-up strike, planned to depart early afternoon. Unbeknownst to them, the biggest Fifth Air Force raid against Rabaul of the war was incoming. The raid would see every available Zero-sen scrambled to contest an armada of low-level Mitchell bombers and their escorting Lightnings. Earning the American nickname "Bloody Tuesday," the maelstrom about to ensue forced cancellation of the second Torokina beachhead strike.

The first blow to Rabaul was struck by medium-level bombing attacks by Liberators. Low-level Mitchell strafers from Dobodura followed. These crews had gone through an elongated process to get here. First briefed in Port Moresby before staging to Dobodura, they had been there two days waiting for the weather to clear. The Mitchells toted both phosphorous and general-purpose bombs, painting at times a dramatic backdrop of white octopus tentacles as they went. Following widespread combat, the Mitchells' gunners claimed 26 fighters shot down, and the destruction of 16 aircraft on the ground, along with another ten floatplanes and flying boats moored in the harbor. The Lightnings separately claimed 29 aerial victories, totaling 55 American aerial kills, but this number was a gross exaggeration. In fact, the Americans paid an appalling price. They lost 11 Mitchells and crews from the 3rd, 38th, and 345th Bombardment Groups, and nine Lightnings from the 8th, 49th, and 475th Fighter Groups, a combined total of 20 aircraft. Furthermore, many participant airframes were subsequently written off at Dobodura on return.

Several enraged Zero-sen pilots pursued the retreating Mitchells at low level, later detailed by 38th Bombardment Group Mitchell pilot Lt Cal Gillespie:

We had Zero-sen off to the right and left, but my gunner does not fire at them. He is out of ammo also. I hope they are too, and they must be for they try no hostile moves. They get closer as if to join our formation. Nobody is firing. Dammed if they aren't showing off now for they do some barrel rolls. I feel like trying one also but forget that stupidity instantly. The Japanese pilot to my right waves goodbye and I finger my nose at him. He breaks hard right and heads back to Rabaul.

Phosphorous bombs dropped from Fifth Air Force strafer B-25Ds explode on the northwest end of Lakunai airfield on November 2. The township and main wharf area of Rabaul are to the far left.

Several Zero-sen losses were unwitnessed by their own side, as many chose to hound the Mitchells a long way out to sea, and it appears several were dispatched by Mitchell gunners during this last phase. These were carrier pilots; no land-based Zero-sen had previously engaged in this type of modus operandi, and besides, the activity is reflected in the day's operational logs. Instead of 55 aerial kills from the battle as claimed, the Americans in fact scored 19, thus claiming three times as many aircraft as they actually shot down. The breakdown was 14 pilots and 20 Zero-sen; Admiral Ozawa's carrier Zero-sen units lost nine pilots and 12 Zero-sen, 201 Ku and 204 Ku lost four pilots and seven Zero-sen, and 253 Ku based at Tobera lost one pilot and one Zero-sen. These loss figures include six Zero-sen lost to takeoff accidents. A handful of Japanese pilots successfully bailed out. To balance this fiction, Japanese claims were even more fanciful and verged on the hysterical: 36 Mitchells and 85 Lightnings, a total of 121 against the 20 aircraft lost.

This raid was unique for several reasons, including the strafers' approach from the north after conducting a feint toward New Ireland. The first alarm was raised by a 501 Ku Judy flown by pilot FPO2c Kawashima Yoshimi, who was on his second patrol of the day from Vunakanau. After departing at 1100hrs, Kawashima spotted the incoming formation, which he estimated contained 50 low-level Mitchells. His observer radioed the sighting at 1225hrs, which sent Rabaul into a frenzy. A visual sighting from the entrenched spotting position on

Fifth Air Force B-25D strafers pass over two merchantmen in Rabaul harbor on November 2. The wakes from two 500lb bombs underline the challenges in hitting a ship even from low level

top of the Mother volcano confirmed Rabaul's worst fears. The position afforded an expansive 360-degree view from 2,000ft above sea level. Meanwhile, another outgunned Judy pilot dropped two 30kg (66lb) phosphorous bombs into the Mitchell formation as they closed on Rabaul, with "unknown results."

Zuikaku got 21 Zero-sen airborne but lost FPO1c Yoshida Saburo to combat and another pilot who went missing. One *Zuikaku* Zero-sen was strafed on the ground while taxiing and burned, while its pilot ran for safety. Another *Zuikaku* Zero-sen collided during takeoff with a land-based fighter also trying to depart. Both fighters were badly damaged in ensuing crash landings, but incredibly both pilots were uninjured. The last *Zuikaku* Zero landed back at Vunakanau at 1320hrs.

Twenty-five *Shokaku* A6M2s led by Lt Satao Masao, the second-most senior carrier fighter pilot after Lt Notomi Kenjiro, lost two Zero-sen to combat. One of these was division officer Lt (jg) Miyabe Kazunori, who died at Rabaul's Navy hospital the next morning from wounds sustained in the fight. Three *Shokaku* Zero-sen failed to return. *Zuiho* launched a dozen Zero-sen, of which one failed to return. The luckiest escape of the day belongs to *Zuiho*'s No. 3 *shotaicho* Lt Fukui Yoshio, who intercepted a low-flying Mitchell as it crossed the harbor shoreline. Immediately after opening fire, his fighter was set ablaze by attacking Lightnings which had boxed him in just above the treeline. Climbing into his attacker's gun sights was a bad option; Fukui's best escape was to bail out at low-level, dangerous at the best of times. Nonetheless, Fukui's injuries were limited to burns to his right foot as he ambulated to the nearest road. The energetic Fukui was back in the cockpit three days later.

During this headlong rush, every one of Rabaul's land-based fighter units put Zero-sen in the air too: 201 Ku launched 21 fighters, losing two to combat, and another was written off at Vunakanau on return, its pilot slightly wounded; 204 Ku put up 17, but two were gunned down. Another 204 Ku pair was damaged on takeoff and sidelined; 253 Ku launched 19 Zero-sen and lost one to combat. Based at Tobera, this Zero-sen unit was then the best-equipped fighter unit at Rabaul, able to launch missions of 30 Zero-sen, including the latest A6M5 Model 52s. *Hikotaicho* Lt-Cdr Okamoto Harutoshi had been the one to raise the alarm with his pilots, having received a phone call from the Vunakanau central communications unit.

After the dust settled from the American raid, the first Operation *Ro-Go* attack by Kates was put into place. Rather than carry torpedoes, six *Shokaku* Kates, led by Lt Ono Hiroji, each toted four 60kg (132lb) bombs, an ineffectual ordnance to use against shipping offshore Torokina. Their failure to load torpedoes is unclear; perhaps it is aligned with the consideration that the Type 91 aerial torpedoes required wooden fins to be added to stabilize in the slipstream when slung underneath the Kate's fuselage. Perhaps Vunakanau's workshops had been sufficiently interrupted to delay production of the required fins in time. Regardless, Ono's flight plan was up against weather that had worsened considerably since the relatively clear conditions of the morning attack. After departing Vunakanau at 1705hrs, these Kates had trouble finding anything, let alone shipping, in the dark gloomy weather. At 2235hrs five Kates landed back at Vunakanau, with Ono's left-hand wingman having disappeared on the return journey.

That night, as the tired Japanese crews tried to sleep, Beauforts bombarded Tobera airfield, home to 253 Ku's Zero-sen. These Beauforts were a composite formation of RAAF No. 6 Squadron from Vivigani on Goodenough Island, and Nos 8 and 100 Squadrons based at Kiriwina. Six No. 8 Squadron Beauforts attacked first at 2200hrs, but their bombs fell wide. The other two squadrons attacked in the darkness of early next morning, with three of 14 Beauforts aborting with mechanical troubles. One was circling at 0300hrs, trying to locate Tobera, when a lit flare path and green flashing light encouraged him to approach as a friendly aircraft. Capitalizing on this case of obvious mistaken identity, the Beaufort dived and made a run along the runway, dropping bombs along the way. Another Beaufort was attacked over Wide Bay by a 251 Ku Irving night-fighter, forcing him to jettison bombs and return to base. While the rest of the RAAF Beauforts loitered over Rabaul, that same night Buka-based Jakes from both 938 Ku and 958 Ku raided Mono Island, ambling over the target area in the early hours of November 3. Each dropped two 60kg (132lb) bombs, which did little damage but prevented a restful night.

November 3

When the next day dawned, determined Japanese commanders authorized Operation *Ro-Go* to recommence. The morning of November 3 broke into clear weather, and the sun shone over the Torokina beachhead, attended by scattered small cumulus and unlimited visibility. Eight *Zuikaku* Vals were loaded at Vunakanau, this time each with more potent 250kg (550lb) bombs, with the intention of dropping them into American ships reported in the vicinity of Mono Island. Fighter and protection echelons totaling 45 Zero-sen (17 *Zuikaku*, 16 *Shokaku*, 12 *Zuiho*) would escort Val dive-bombers. These would be accompanied by one *Shokaku* Judy, later reported in the VMF-211 contact report as a solitary "Tony." Led by Zero pilot Lt Notomi Kenjiro, the plan was for the Vals to bomb the ships, and later strafe them with Zero-sen if the opportunity presented itself.

Following a 1000hrs departure, around midday the Zero-sen were surprised by two divisions of VMF-211 Corsairs patrolling the area, comprising seven fighters, as one Corsair had returned to Barakoma early with mechanical troubles. Eight Munda-based 44th Fighter

Model 21 *Zuiho* Zero-sen defending Rabaul from low-level B-25Ds of the 345th Bombardment Group

Commander of 498th Bombardment Squadron, Major Benjamin Fridge, leads B-25D Mitchell "Red Wrath" low over Rabaul township and harbor on November 2, 1943 before being attacked by Zero-sen including several from *Zuiho*. The Mitchell's mission was to drop phosphorous bombs into shore installations and the town to create a smokescreen to hamper Japanese AA gunners.

Jim Laurier

Squadron P-40Fs were also on patrol, but were too far south to engage. The Corsairs and Zero-sen met at 20,000ft over Empress Augusta Bay, while the Vals some 5,000ft below broke off to bomb the beachheads near Torokina, where they incurred little damage. This skirmish resulted in an even score of two aircraft lost per side – VMF-211 Corsair pilots Major George Moffat and 1/Lt Robert Hatfield both went MIA with no clue to their demise. *Zuikaku* lost one Val and one Zero-sen to the Corsairs, flown respectively by pilots FPO1c Ogura Shinichi and FPO1c Aomi Hisashi. Since none of the five returned Corsair pilots claimed to have attacked Vals, it appears possible that either or both Moffat and Hatfield did so, and lost their lives in the process. For the Japanese, however, the raid was a waste of time, progressing no campaign objectives, regardless of the ornate claims of the Zero-sen pilots that they somehow downed ten Corsairs.

November 4

On Thursday November 4 the weather around Cape Gazelle and the Rabaul area was thick with cloud, squalls, and rain, to the extent it was obvious no attacks could proceed. That mid-morning, eight *Zuikaku* Zero-sen nonetheless flew a two-hour patrol around the Gazelle Peninsula; eight more from *Zuiho* also did so, separately. The weather had cleared sufficiently by early afternoon for a *Zuikaku* Judy to attempt a shipping reconnaissance, but it was back on the ground after an unfruitful three-hour flight. Just after midday, 15 *Zuiho* Zero-sen attempted a CAP leaving just after midday, but after clawing their way through a littoral of squalls were back on the ground half an hour later. *Shokaku*'s Zero-sen were the most active that day, conducting four separate patrols of around an hour each, in flights of seven and eight Zero-sen.

First Rabaul attack – November 5

A curveball was now thrown into the equation by the IJN when, early on November 4, a reconnaissance Liberator discovered a flotilla of heavy cruisers heading for Rabaul, recorded in the subsequent USAAF report thus: "a large enemy task force comprised of five heavy cruisers, three light cruisers and five destroyers, with four freighters and two corvettes, is proceeding to the Rabaul area from Truk."

With his mind focused on the serious situation unfolding at Torokina, Admiral Koga was determined to rectify matters. Accordingly, he ordered Admiral Kurita Takeo to destroy the US forces in Empress Augusta Bay. Kurita had dispatched his 8th Fleet cruisers from Truk to do the job, including *Maya*, *Takao*, *Atago*, *Suzuya*, *Chikuma*, *Chokai*, and *Mogami*, escorted by light cruiser *Noshiro*, four destroyers, and two trailing oilers, *Nichiei Maru* and *Nissho Maru*. This flotilla was to join two cruisers, *Myoko* and *Haguro*, already anchored at Rabaul. The resultant task force would be sufficiently substantive to break through USN ships around Empress Augusta Bay, and then proceed to destroy any merchantmen offshore the landing, and heavily shell the area. The fate of these cruisers would become central to the outcome of Operation *Ro-Go*.

However, from the start few things fell Kurita's way. While en route from Truk, he was informed that his two accompanying oilers had been disabled by a dawn air attack, about 130 miles west of Kavieng. Conducted by Guadalcanal-based B-24 Liberators, a follow-up bombing attack against *Nissho Maru* killed nine sailors and wounded 14 more. Kurita sent cruiser *Chokai* with destroyer *Suzunami* to tow the oilers back to Truk.

Nonetheless, the arrival of Kurita's cruisers at Rabaul suddenly placed the entire Bougainville operation at risk. Luckily, Admiral "Bull" Halsey could muster two aircraft carriers at short notice, consisting of *Saratoga* (the oldest carrier in USN service) and light carrier *Princeton*, supported by two cruisers and nine destroyers. Both carriers had supported

A JAAF 14th Sentai Ki-21 Sally bomber similar to the one seen here was shot down during the November 5 Rabaul raid in Rapopo's circuit area by a Hellcat. Six *Zuiho* Kates returning from Kavieng delayed their return to Vunakanau when warned by radio of the strike in progress.

the Torokina landing only three days before with the air strikes against the Buka area, and were currently refueling offshore Guadalcanal. Halsey's staff officers worked around the clock to assemble a plan to hit Simpson Harbour with a carrier strike against the newly arrived cruisers. Although feasible, it was a dangerous gamble. Despite Kenney's claim that his November 2 air strike had "neutralized" Rabaul, more realistic USN intelligence officers assessed otherwise. They judged Rabaul's fighter inventory at around 150 aircraft, a credible estimate. The combined projected air power of both USN carriers was fewer than 100 aircraft. Furthermore, launching all carrier air assets meant leaving the task force without air cover, anathematic to USN doctrine. To cover this contingency, continuous fighter cover would be furnished, rotating formations of 56 *Munda* and *Ondonga*-based fighters from 0548hrs to 1813hrs. At least, that was the plan; however, things did not turn out that way. To add to the risk calculus was the fact that the short range of the carriers' air power meant the carriers would have to stand-off well north for launch, parallel to Bougainville, and thus within range of Rabaul's Kates, Vals and torpedo-equipped Betty bombers.

All these sobering considerations could not avoid the conclusion that an air strike was the only way to stop Kurita's cruisers. Fifth Air Force strafer Mitchells had proven bombs impotent against such vessels only a few days ago, so torpedoes and dive-bombers would have to do the job. With no easy choice to make, Halsey ordered the strike "go." Admiral Frederick Sherman, former skipper of carrier USS *Lexington*, guided a quickly assembled TF38 at 29 knots toward the launch area, screened by overcast. The fleet sailed hard in order to reach their designated launch area by dawn. This USN operation ordered at short notice had accumulated many moving parts, and required careful coordination. Its working mechanisms were given the bland name of "Plan 17."

Ever vigilant of another US air strike, Rabaul's reconnaissance routines were joined by First Carrier Division assets. At 0855hrs a *Shokaku* Judy commanded by observer Lt Kibayashi Satoshi found Sherman's task force making solid headway 150 nautical miles from Cape St. George, but misidentified both carriers as battleships. Separately, a *Zuikaku* Judy submitted its own report five minutes later, this time confirming the presence of two aircraft carriers. While Rabaul was in the process of assembling an air strike and preparing for the worst, the air-raid alarm sounded at 0915hrs.

With USS *Saratoga* as Sherman's flagship, a dozen other warships in a circular formation guarded it and carrier USS *Princeton*. At 0855hrs USS *Princeton* headed into wind at 30 knots and prepared to launch its aircraft, concluding its send-off of seven VC-23 TBFs

NEW BRITAIN

NEW

SOLOMON SEA

Operation *Ro-Go* – Japanese attacks:
November 1–11, 1943

and 19 VF-23 F6F Hellcats at 0938hrs. At 1010hrs USS *Saratoga* completed its launch of 33 VF-12 Hellcats led by Commander Joseph Clifton, 16 VT-12 Avengers led by Lt-Cdr Robert Harrington, and 22 VB-12 SBDs led by Lt-Cdr James Newell. After the launches were complete, TF38 reduced speed to 20 knots. Thus, a total of 97 aircraft headed for Rabaul: 52 F6F Hellcats, 23 TBF Avengers, and 22 SBD-5 Dauntless dive-bombers. *Saratoga* air commander of CAG-12, Commander Henry Caldwell, would direct the overall strike from a command TBF.

The prevailing wind over Simpson Harbour that morning was south/southeast, aligning all anchored ships along that wind vector's azimuth. Standard modus operandi was for torpedo bombers to parallel the target ship's length, then turn toward the ship to launch torpedoes. Dive-bombers dove on the ship along its length to maximize their chances. The targets were neatly laid out for the attackers; when IJN ships dropped anchor at Rabaul, they did so in predetermined and orderly positions. These were referenced using fixes of 1,000 and 1,500m distances relative to prominent positions, especially the Beehive (named "Nakajima" or Central Island). Such anchoring sequences were strictly observed.

Coordinating the USN squadrons was *Saratoga* air commander of CAG-12, Commander Henry Caldwell. From wide circles at 10,000ft, Caldwell directed the shipping attacks after leading the attackers down St. George's Channel until just north of Crater Peninsula. From there the formations wheeled left to fly over Simpson Harbour from the north, allowing the attackers to escape over the harbor mouth. Caldwell's flyers arrived shortly after the Japanese cruisers had anchored; as they approached, some Japanese warships had already commenced refueling to prepare for an assault against Torokina planned that night.

The morning reconnaissance reports from the *Zuikaku* and *Shokaku* Judys had placed Rabaul on full alert, but with barely sufficient time to prepare. It was the lookout position atop Mother volcano that confirmed the incoming expected raid. As the USN aircraft approached the harbor, the first Japanese fighters to launch were Zero-sen from *Zuiho* and *Shokaku*. Initially these loitered some distance from the USN formations, holding off engagement until the USN aircraft fragmented prior to commencing their attack. As they did this, every antiaircraft gun ashore and afloat opened up on the USN formations. The Japanese fighters cautiously remained outside the flak screen, but they had misjudged the enemy's movements, for the attackers commenced their tasks regardless of the flak. The Zero-sen went after them after bombs and torpedoes had been dropped, chasing the Americans, which then bolted across the harbor and headed for home. The TBFs, last to attack, bore the brunt of the Zero-sen. Then, unexpectedly, there was another surprise when the higher Zero-sen formations broke off their pursuit to deal with another threat, this time courtesy of Kenney's Fifth Air Force: 27 B-24s escorted by 67 P-38s. The Liberators' bombs struck the main wharf area at 1225hrs. These intruders were met with only light fighter opposition, as the USN raid had already diverted most Japanese attention.

Meanwhile, back at TF38, it was soon after launch that the constant air cover from land-based fighters started going awry. Capricious weather was encountered by most flights, often preventing three flights of eight fighters each from locating the ships. In the event no enemy contact threatened the carriers, and the only damage to the escorts occurred when two Corsairs were lightly damaged returning in the dark. Nonetheless, nine patrolling VF-33 Hellcats from Munda managed to find USS *Princeton* and commenced landing on its deck at 1110hrs. Safely aboard, they refueled in an orderly manner then returned to their base.

Japanese resistance

Although *Zuiho* division officer Lt Sato Masao is recorded as mission commander for the carrier Zero-sen battle of November 5, this entry is a formality. In reality, the carrier units had no time to coordinate their fight, let alone coordinate with Rabaul's land-based Zero-sen units.

Planes from USS *Saratoga* and *Princeton* attack Rabaul's fleet on November 5. This high azimuth looking westwards was taken from a *Saratoga* TBF. Landmarks include Tavurvur Crater in the middle left, Sulphur Point to the lower right, and Matupi Island with causeway to the center right. The entrance to Simpson Harbour is out of sight to the left.

In fact, 201 Ku did not launch their 13 Zero-sen from Lakunai until 1130hrs, about 15 minutes after the USN squadrons appeared, such was the nature of the confusion. A total of 86 Zero-sen rose to defend Rabaul. In addition to 201 Ku who lost FPO1c Miyamoto Yoshio in the fight, 204 Ku placed 11 fighters in the air, and 253 Ku 15. *Shokaku* had 17 in the game, and both *Zuiho* and *Zuikaku* launched 15 fighters each. The *Zuikaku* contingent, based at Tobera alongside 253 Ku, lost FPO1c Nishimura Hiroshi, while *Zuiho* lost FCPO Minato Kosaku, with another unidentified *Zuiho* pilot seriously wounded from burns. Separately, a 204 Ku Zero-sen was totaled upon return to Lakunai, badly wounding its pilot.

Somewhere in this widespread combat was also a contingent of five 501 Ku Judys which launched from Vunakanau alongside the first carrier Zero-sen. They dropped 30kg (66lb) aerial phosphorous bombs into the USN formations, which looked impressive but did no damage. This unit lost pilot FCPO Hamoto Ichirou and his observer to USN fighters.

Thus the complete tally of IJN aircrew lost was five killed and two badly wounded, with one Judy and five Zero-sen airframes lost. The JAAF also contributed several 68th Sentai Vunakanau-based Ki-61 Tonys without loss, scoring several hits on the Hellcats. The last IJN defender touched down at 1300hrs. However, there is an additional Japanese casualty, incidental to the tally – a JAAF 14th Sentai Ki-21 Sally bomber unfortunate enough to be in Rapopo's circuit area when a fleeing Hellcat diverted its guns to bring it down into palm trees. Another curiosity was the delayed arrival at Vunakanau of six *Zuiho* Kates returning from a brief deployment to Kavieng. Warned by radio of the strike in progress, they held off almost until the last attacker had gone, landing just after 1230hrs.

Given their offensive role, combined USN aircraft losses were relatively light: ten aircraft, including five TBFs, four F6Fs and one SBD, with one 9th Fighter Squadron P-38 shot down during the USAAF follow-on raid. At 1640hrs, after both carriers had retrieved their last aircraft from offshore Bougainville, TF38 made fast passage southwards to get away.

Now we turn to analyzing the main objective of neutralizing the cruisers. During the attack, many fired their main batteries as a deterrent in their rushed defense. The rationale was that the impressive blast, visual and otherwise, would constitute a formidable preventive. Two cruisers

VB-9 SBDs about to launch from the deck of USS *Essex* for the November 11 Rabaul strike.

had been in the process of refueling, making it harder for them to escape, became the focus of disproportionate attention. One of these was *Maya*, which took a bomb on its aircraft deck above engine room #3. This started a major fire below, killing 70 sailors and injuring 60. Similarly, while refueling from oiler *Kokuyo Maru*, *Atago* incurred hull damage from three near-misses.

Saratoga's SBDs placed a 500lb bomb between *Mogami*'s two front turrets, decommissioning both, and causing a fierce fire which killed 19 sailors and wounded 37. A resulting explosion removed a major portion of *Mogami*'s starboard bow above the waterline, and although it could still sail, the damage hampered the cruiser's speed to 12 knots. On the other side of the harbor, two 500lb bombs holed *Takao* below its waterline, damaging its steering and killing 23 sailors. *Chikuma* received a near-miss to the starboard catapult from a *Saratoga* SBD, decommissioning a torpedo mount, causing flooding, and wounding three sailors. Three near-misses flooded several of *Atago*'s boiler room compartments and engine room #1, wounding 64 and killing 22 crew. Significantly, the casualties included the captain, IJN Captain Nakaoka Nobuki, impacted by shrapnel as he was shouting orders from the bridge.

From this inventory of affliction, the only cruiser left undamaged was *Suzuya*. Light cruisers *Agano* and *Noshiro* were also hit, as were two destroyers, including one by a dud torpedo. Although the USN air strike had not sunk one ship, this was not the point; the purpose of neutralizing the threat posed by the cruisers had been well-achieved. Five heavy cruisers were damaged, three to the extent they would require dockyard repairs. Admiral Kurita had no choice but to cancel his naval offensive. The growing Torokina beachhead and ongoing northern Solomons operations had been spared. That night Kurita started sending his ambulatory cruisers back to Truk or Japan for repair, never to return to Rabaul.

A retaliatory debacle – November 5

With American danger still lurking offshore in the shape of two carriers, it was imperative they be found. Ashore at 8th Fleet Headquarters, an unsettled Admiral Kurita conferred with Admiral Kusaka Jinichi to discuss the best way to retaliate. What followed arguably constitutes the biggest lost opportunity to beset the IJN in the South Seas. Unbeknownst to both belligerents was that a trivial USN flotilla comprising patrol boat *PT-167*, infantry

landing craft *LCI-70*, and tank landing craft *LCT-68* was in the process of sailing from Torokina to Treasury Island to deliver supplies. They pulled anchor at Torokina at 1500hrs and set off in fair weather, although a high overcast persisted.

Events as they now unfolded almost beggar belief, highlighting the degree to which several anxious carrier aircrews were inexperienced, leading to rash decisions. It is hard to imagine how any IJN aviator, even in fading light, could confuse this modest collective for two aircraft carriers surrounded by a task force, but this is exactly what happened.

It will be recalled that Lt Kibayashi Satoshi's *Shokaku* Judy had been first to find TF38 earlier that morning but had misidentified the two carriers as battleships. A *Zuikaku* Judy had shortly thereafter submitted they were in fact two aircraft carriers, a fact borne out by Kurita's shattered cruiser fleet, now ambulating around the harbor. The first glaring task was to relocate the offending US task force, and the first attempt to do this was made by another solitary *Zuikaku* Judy. This departed Vunakanau at 1355hrs, barely an hour after the dust had settled from the USN attack. It headed southeast and an hour later its pilot WO I'ida Uetada counted two aircraft carriers surrounded by nine more substantive ships offshore Bougainville's southeastern coast. He kept his distance while transmitting regular reports of fleet vectors before retiring to Vunakanau at 1830hrs. Separately, another *Zuikaku* Judy flown by WO Yoshikawa Takeshi departed Vunakanau at 1520hrs to take over from I'ida. However, Yoshikawa's subsequent sighting report made at 1620hrs only served to confuse Rabaul. Instead of finding TF38, Yoshikawa's observer reported a group of three ships and returned to Vunakanau at 1700hrs, a good hour and a half before I'ida.

Meanwhile, at Vunakanau the task of finding and destroying the carriers had been handed to *Zuikaku* division officer Lt Kiyomiya Tsuyoshi. Kates were the optimal choice of weapon; not only did they have the capacity to stay aloft for a long time, but their carrier crews were best trained for oceanic navigation, especially since darkness was encroaching. First, however, Kiyomiya needed to resolve the two ship sightings in approximately the same area; were they the same ships or two different groups? Aware of high cloud cover which would produce a

The Australian Treasury building and post office just before Japanese occupation, and later on 8th Fleet base headquarters. Both these buildings had been badly damaged by Allied air attacks by the time of Operation *Ro-Go*.

A wounded AO3 Kenneth Bratton being extracted from Lt-Cdr Robert Harrington's VT-19 TBF #19 aboard USS *Saratoga* on November 5, 1943, resulting in one of the best-known photos of the Pacific War. When Harrington started orbiting Simpson Harbour escorted by two Hellcats, several Zero pilots assessed that the trio was important and shot up all three aircraft.

particularly dark night, he knew this matter needed to be resolved.

With evidence pointing to another flotilla in the same vicinity as the main target, Kiyomiya sent two separate pairs of *Zuikaku* and *Zuiho* Kates on a "search and destroy" mission. These were divided into two pairs, and at 1617hrs team *Zuikaku* launched two Kates commanded by observers Leading Aircraftsman Itokawa Morio and FPO2c Yamazaki Saburo. They split up and separately reported *PT-167*'s collective of three vessels 175 nautical miles distant, then, ten minutes later, a larger flotilla 200 nautical miles distant, being TF38. This pair returned to Vunakanau in the dark at 2150hrs. The second pair of Kates from *Zuiho* launched half an hour after the first, finding the smaller flotilla at 2000hrs, then diverting to Kavieng in pitch darkness, where they touched down at 2345hrs. None of these Kates conducted attacks.

At 1815hrs an unidentified aircraft flew eastwards past *PT-167* and friends, about two miles shy of them. It flashed a red light only once but maintained course before disappearing to the east. This was Itokawa in the first *Zuikaku* Kate, whose radio operator transmitted the small flotilla's location five minutes later at 1820hrs. Armed with all the above position reports, *Zuikaku* division officer Lt Kiyomiya Tsuyoshi assembled 15 Kates: seven from *Zuikaku*, four from *Shokaku*, and four of the six *Zuiho* Kates which had returned to Vunakanau from Kavieng just after the USN raid. Kiyomiya launched the decisive strike force into two groups; the four *Zuiho* Kates left at 1715hrs, followed by the *Shokaku* and *Zuikaku* Kates 15 minutes later. The two groups soon formed up in their hunt for TF38, which had commenced fleeing south at 1640hrs. Not surprisingly in the fading light of overcast, Kiyomiya had trouble finding them. Finally, at 1910hrs Kiyomiya had a confirmed sighting and descended his 15 Kates rapidly for an attack position. Below, *PT-167*'s log notes that by 1915hrs the supply flotilla had steadied course and was well underway. The sun had just set, making it dark eastwards, with fading twilight to the west. Without any warning, suddenly Kiyomiya's 15 Kates appeared low on the western horizon at around 200ft.

The first flight of three Kates accelerated toward *PT-167*, which opened fire with its machine gun, the gun crew noting the lead Kate headed directly at them barely 20ft above water level. As proven over the years in times of both conflict and peace, the enemy of every aviator is an invisible wire strung between two objects. As the Kate passed low overhead, its wing caught on the vessel's radio antenna, causing it to crash into the sea and badly shaking *PT-167*. This collision marked the instant demise of Lt Kiyomiya Tsuyoshi and his crew of three. Kiyomiya had launched his torpedo at *PT-167*, but it did not explode and instead passed cleanly through the bow of the patrol boat's wooden hull, smashing a 6x2ft hole clean through *PT-167*'s bow. Pieces of torpedo fin and rudder lay scattered about the deck; a later assessment concluded that the torpedo had been delivered at short distance. It had then driven through the hull before it had a chance to arm itself.

A few minutes later, the second flight of Kates attacked from the same direction but lined up further astern. The 20mm gunner firing from the PT's fantail saw his shots hit home on one attacking Kate which burst into flames and crashed, so close to the port quarter in fact that sailors crouching on the stern were drenched by the splash. Its torpedo ran under the fantail and disappeared to port. This second crash marked the end for *Zuikaku*'s FPO1c Nishiyama Hisao and crew of three.

As darkness fell swiftly, the other Kates continued with more unsuccessful attacks, but by then it had become sufficiently dark that only the blue exhaust flames of the torpedo bombers could be seen. Return gunfire claimed no more victims. When the Japanese had departed, *PT-167* drew alongside *LCI-70*, aboard which, it was soon discovered, an unexploded torpedo had lodged itself in the engine room. *LCI-70* was later towed back to base by *LCT-68*. Meanwhile, *PT-167* returned to Torokina carrying several injured crew, where it berthed at midnight.

The bow of *PT-167* showing the hole left from the torpedo dropped by Lt Kiyomiya Tsuyoshi's Kate, which passed cleanly through the wooden hull during the twilight of November 5. Kiyomiya hit the PT's aerial during the attack run causing it to crash into the water.

Eleven Kates landed at Vunakanau at 2110hrs. The *Zuiho* crews waited in vain for their second flight to materialize; however, these two Kates had been shot down over the target, the first flown by Leading Airman Taguchi Goro, the other commanded by Leading Airman Kobayashi Kiyoto. The fifth of eight children of a Hiroshima family, 21-year-old Taguchi's first run over the target had been wide so he turned for another pass. His Kate was then shot down by AA fire during his final approach to target at a few hundred feet altitude. He was kept afloat by his Kapok jacket and kept treading water until 1500hrs hours the following afternoon, when he was rescued by a USN destroyer. Taguchi spent the rest of the war as a POW. His two crewmen, however, had gone down with the aircraft.

Back at Vunakanau the surviving Kate crews claimed to have sunk one large and one medium aircraft carrier, along with two cruisers and two destroyers. In fact, they had sunk nothing, and instead fruitlessly attacked a patrol boat flotilla of three small vessels, losing four Kates in the process. Even discounting the benefit of hindsight, such extravagant claims are as difficult to understand then as they are now. Their claims meant that Operation *Ro-Go* had just lurched from mediocrity into fiction.

RAAF night attack – November 5

Now we turn to the efforts of the RAAF to counter Operation *Ro-Go*, often overlooked. The RAAF also had a torpedo bomber unit in-theater, operating Bristol Beauforts. The obsolete design was heavily loaded when carrying a torpedo. There had been considerable criticism, even within the RAAF itself, of the Beaufort's role as a torpedo-carrying aircraft. A successful large-scale attack on a lucrative target such as that presented by Rabaul would boost its prestige as a tactical weapon, and perhaps sway RAAF command to retain the costly torpedo-bomber training base at RAN Nowra, located on the New South Wales coast south of Sydney.

RAAF No. 9 Operational Group housed all RAAF units in the South West Pacific Area (SWPA). Its commanding officer was Air Commodore Eric "Joe" Hewitt, who seized an opportunity to follow the success of the day assault against Rabaul's shipping with a night torpedo attack against Simpson Harbour. This would be an interim mission – Hewitt planned a much larger one for November 8 to showcase what the Beaufort could do. For this evening, four RAAF No. 8 Squadron Beauforts would target two identified oilers and other enemy

Medical corpsmen about to remove casualties from TBF #19 flown by CAG-12 leader Lt-Cdr Robert Harrington from USS *Saratoga* on November 5, 1943, after the left main gear failed to lower on return from Rabaul. Gunner AO3 Ken Bratton was wounded, and photographer PM1 Paul Barnett was killed when the torpedo bomber was shot up by Zero-sen. Harrington is climbing from the cockpit.

shipping anchored in Keravia Bay, while four more Beauforts from RAAF No. 100 Squadron would simultaneously bomb Vunakanau airfield just opposite the same bay. While Kiyomiya's 11 surviving Kates were making their way back to Rabaul, Squadron Leader Noel Quinn led these eight Beauforts toward Rabaul that evening from Kiriwina. After one aborted, at 1040hrs Quinn opened the attack by descending his flight of four and lining up a ship in Keravia Bay from a height of 150ft. After releasing the torpedo, a searchlight blinded him so he could not see where it struck. The second torpedo curved left and missed its target. The third was aimed at a cruiser, but despite post-mission optimism it too missed. Meanwhile, the No. 100 Squadron Beauforts got to work over Vunakanau but damaged little.

Search and precaution – November 6

Having paid such a heavy price the previous day and three days before that, the possibility of another carrier or air strike had Rabaul on full alert. As soon as possible it launched numerous resources to try to locate and, if possible, attack the task force. Searches were made over the ocean area north of Bougainville and southeast of the same island towards Kiriwina. American and RNZAF fighters based at Ondonga maintained six patrols over Empress Augusta Bay throughout the day from dawn until dusk.

First patrol was a mixed flight of four *Zuiho*, *Shokaku*, and *Zuikaku* Kates led by *Zuikaku* division officer Lt Matsukawa Mutsuro, who split the searchers into two pairs. The area was, again, riddled with squalls which reduced visibility. Matsukawa radioed Rabaul at 0735hrs that he had found four enemy ships east of Bougainville, and the *Zuiho/Shokaku* pair confirmed the sighting at 0845hrs. Matsukawa's transmission was his last, for his Kate with three men aboard was never seen again. They were not a victim of US gunfire, so it appears they had become yet another statistic claimed by capricious weather.

Fourteen VF-17 Corsairs escorted six 42nd Bombardment Group B-25Ds, which attacked three ships close offshore Buka at 0730hrs and sank two. A division of four returning Corsairs led by Lt Merl Davenport encountered a solitary Betty northeast of Torokina. Davenport's fighters took turns to drive the Betty into the sea in flames. This one-sided fight saw the end of 751 Ku pilot FPO1c O'ota Kazuyoshi and his crew of five, which had departed Vunakanau at 0415hrs to conduct an extended patrol of the Torokina area.

Meanwhile, back at Rabaul and separate to all other aerial operations, defensive countermeasures saw many busy Zero-sen that day. Three precautionary fighter scrambles launched in response to false sightings of enemy aircraft. First were 11 *Zuiho* Zero-sen, which scuttled from Vunakanau at 0805hrs but were recalled after only 25 minutes airborne. Next was a composite formation of 28 201 Ku and 204 Ku Zero-sen led by 201 Ku pilot Lt (jg) O'oba Yoshio, which dashed out from Lakunai at 1330hrs. They were recalled only 40 minutes later; however, three more scrambles of 11 Zero-sen patrolled Rabaul skies for the day's remainder, the last of which was an extended three-hour patrol led by 201 Ku pilot WO Kibayashi Itsuo, returning at dusk at 1850hrs. The Japanese were taking no chances.

At 1200hrs a *Shokaku* Judy launched, and not quite three hours later, after giving wide berth to a pesky P-38, reported locating two cruisers and seven destroyers followed by a separate flotilla of eight ships nearby. This was a big find; however, unbeknownst to its crew, its radio report failed to reach Rabaul. Nonetheless, the sighting was quickly passed to IJN commanders when it returned to Vunakanau at 1630hrs. At 1802hrs two pairs of *Zuiho* Kates set off to find the enemy ships but again were thwarted by the weather after several hours of searching. They returned to Vunakanau just before midnight.

Two failed strikes – November 6

Determined to find and attack the reported ships, it was decided to deploy First Carrier Division Vals and Kates to do the job. At 2040hrs 14 Vals led by *Zuikaku* division officer Lt Hira Kunikiyo (ten *Shokaku*, four *Zuikaku*) set out in the gloomy conditions to find them. Within barely half an hour they found themselves enveloped in heavy rain and all-embracing darkness. Hira gingerly turned back and skillfully relocated Vunakanau, where all landed safely, having been airborne for just over an hour. In the interim, and hearing nothing from Hira's Vals, at 2110hrs a mixture of 21 Kates (three *Zuiho*, 14 *Shokaku*, and four *Zuikaku*), led by *Shokaku* observer Lt Ono Hiroji, headed out. They too hit the fickle weather, which split the formations, and Ono's Vals did not get back safely to Vunakanau until 0100hrs next morning. While the Vals and Kates were negotiating dark blustery skies, so too were no fewer than 11 958 Ku Jakes. These roamed individually around the same waters, also seeking the ships, departing Rabaul's Malaguna anchorage between 1905hrs and 0150hrs into the early hours of November 7. Pilot FCPO Yamamoto Toshimaru and a crew of three made a precautionary outlanding when they became lost, but later got home safely next day. Down at Buka, 938 Ku Jakes too ran a similar series of night missions, but bombing Torokina with modest payloads. Lack of Japanese success that evening and into the following morning was not for want of trying.

Meanwhile, the US objective at Torokina remained steadfast: to establish a firm foothold over an area sufficient to build a secure airfield complex. Despite Japanese suspicions, there had been no thought given to acquisition of other areas within Bougainville. Around Cape Torokina itself there was only sufficient suitable ground to construct a fighter strip, which by necessity paralleled the coastline. By November 4, lateral roads had been created which ran inland, although swampy ground made the supply of advance units a difficult matter. Patrols had meanwhile pushed in all directions, with the objective of locating new positions to safeguard and extend the perimeter. However, one patrol had proceeded to the village of Piva, some 21 miles north, where a wide plain held promise of a suitable site for the main airfield complex.

NEW BRITAIN

NEW

1

2

SOLOMON SEA

EVENTS

1 Attack 1: Nov 2: Fifth Air Force attacks Rabaul shipping and airfields.
Begins 1230hrs.

2 Attack 2: Nov 5: 19 Hellcats and 7 TBFs deploy from USS *Princeton*, also
33 Hellcats, 16 Avengers, and 22 SBDs from USS *Saratoga* and attack
Rabaul harbor. Begins 1115hrs.

3 Attack 3: Nov 11: Aircraft deployed from USS *Princeton*, USS *Saratoga*,
USS *Essex*, USS *Bunker Hill*, and USS *Independence* attack Rabaul
harbor. Begins 0930hrs.

Operation *Ro-Go* – Allied attacks: November 1–11, 1943

Seabees of the 71st Naval Construction Battalion lay the first perforated steel matting at Torokina airfield in mid-November.

Then, early on the morning of November 6, the Japanese began landing in 21 barges near the mouth of the Laruma River, disgorging an estimated 400 troops, northwest of the landing area at Torokina. They were attacked by US ground forces and air support, including strafing Airacobras, in a series of actions which continued throughout November 7 and 8. It was estimated that over 250 Japanese were killed, and the rest scattered into the jungle.

Against the odds – November 7

At 0900hrs Rabaul's ongoing vigilance was heightened further following receipt of a radio message sent from the 8th Fleet communications station at Buin. It had been relayed from the Shortlands lookout post, a wooden platform built into the top of a high tree, with a challenging almost-vertical ladder whose spotters that early morning noted, "A powerful enemy surface force totaling 23 ships, including two aircraft carriers, has been sighted."

There were no aircraft carriers; these ships were in fact attack and high-speed transports on their way to deliver more supplies to Torokina as part of TF31, guarded by ten destroyers. As they sailed past, these ships logged the Treasury Islands in view at 0400hrs. Previous and later supply convoys would also include slower tank-landing transports (LST) and infantry landing craft (LCI). These LSTs had an unusual defense up their sleeve too; they launched barrage balloons when unloading. This was the first time in the entire Solomons campaign that such ships had been used to make regular supply runs. Nonetheless, the narrow beach continued to impede unloading progress and unloading times took longer than planned.

Due to encroaching weather, it was not until 1423hrs that *Zuikaku* Judy pilot WO Yoshikawa Takeshi finally got airborne and headed for the area around Shortland and Mono Island groups to find the ships. He and his observer scoured the area for more than two hours but all in vain; the visibility was atrocious, and under the circumstances they too were lucky to get back to Rabaul. Given the conditions and the failures of other searchers to get through the previous day, Rabaul shelved all ideas of a strike for the day.

Meanwhile, over at Lakunai, 201 Ku pilot Lt (jg) O'oba Yoshio had organized a patrol of 16 Zero-sen from which they returned at 0950hrs and refueled. Japanese caution was justified, for the reported ships were not the only threat. By the time O'oba's flyers had returned, Kenney's Fifth Air Force had already launched another high-altitude Liberator raid destined for Rabaul. The weather was clearer toward New Guinea, the direction from which a formation of 90th and 43rd Bombardment Group Liberators appeared, escorted by Lightnings from five squadrons: the 9th, 39th, 80th, 431st, and 432nd. These materialized over Rabaul at 20,000ft shortly after midday, where they were greeted by *Zuikaku* division officer Lt Notomi Kenjiro leading 38 Zero-sen from *Zuiho*, *Shokaku*, and *Zuikaku*. Twenty minutes later, 27 more 201 Ku fighters led by Lt (jg) O'oba Yoshio joined in. This widespread fight did not get below 14,000ft, and the Lightnings mostly held the Zero-sen away from the Liberators, which were attacked piecemeal by *Shokaku* Zero-sen.

This was another aerial combat over Rabaul where the Americans came off a poor second, claiming five Zero-sen. In fact, total damage to the Japanese was scattered bullet holes to four airframes, easily fixed. The USAAF lost 80th Fighter Squadron Lightning pilot FO Robert Gentile en route to a weather front; however, four more Lightnings were shot down by Notomi's Zero-sen, the last of which landed at 1400hrs. At Vunakanau, O'oba's and Notomi's excited pilots outdid their American counterparts for inflated claims, claiming one Liberator and 16 Lightnings against an actual score of four Lightnings. Following this big fight, Lt (jg) O'oba Yoshio led a quartet of 201 Ku Zero-sen for a follow-on 1330hrs–1430hrs patrol.

An IJN sailor climbs up toward the tree observation post in the Shortland Islands. This post commanded a view of incoming Allied flights from the direction of the Solomon Islands. It radioed its observations to Buka, which then relayed them to Rabaul.

Notomi lost – November 8

Again and again during Operation *Ro-Go*, unpredictable weather had dictated air movements. However, the forecast this morning looked relatively favorable when, in a repeat of the previous day's warning relayed from 8th Fleet communications center Buin, another Shortlands' shipping sighting was relayed. This time division officer Lt Notomi Kenjiro became preoccupied organizing the carrier contingents into a major strike, involving Vals escorted by Zero-sen. Close coordination was required with two land-based Zero-sen units, 201 Ku and 204 Ku, which would escort the Vals.

There was considerable pressure on the attackers, largely as destroying the incoming materiel aboard the US ships would relieve pressure on the Japanese soldiers delivered by barge on November 6 near the mouth of the Laruma River. At this stage Rabaul was unaware that a series of ground actions which had endured most of the previous day had already either badly scattered or wiped them out.

Before examining this major strike of November 8 – the last major air strike against the beachhead – we turn to the first and curious combat of the day. This occurred when five Ondonga-based VF-17 F4Us escorting B-25s for an early morning shipping strike just

Zuikaku division officer Lt Notomi Kenjiro was lost on November 8 while leading a combined formation of 74 carrier and land-based Zero-sen from 201 Ku, 204 Ku, and carriers *Zuiho*, *Shokaku*, and *Zuikaku*. Notomi was a key and influential strike leader throughout the campaign.

south of Buka persisted northwards. They did so after seven fellow Corsairs turned back due to persistent frontal squalls. These five found no enemy activity, so continued onwards to Buka airfield, where they strafed fighters and men standing around the runway. Lieutenant Commander John Blackburn conducted a side pass against a twin-engine aircraft on final approach – a G3M2 Nell delivering supplies from Rabaul – which crashed and burst into flames.

Meanwhile, back at Rabaul, Notomi's first task was to coordinate the movement of Zero-sen from the land-based and carrier units. The former comprised seven 201 Ku fighters led by Lt (jg) O'oba Yoshio, and 27 from 204 Ku led by Lt (jg) Morita Heitaro. These would join 40 carrier-based Zero-sen, 15 each from *Zuiho* and *Shokaku*, with ten more from *Zuikaku*. This was an impressive overall formation of 74 fighters.

Since arriving at Rabaul, engineers attached to the carrier-based Vals had made time to install center-line ordnance racks to carry 250kg (550lb) bombs, a far more effective weapon than the smaller 60kg (132lb) bombs carried on previous missions. A total of 26 D3A2 Vals, 16 from *Shokaku* and ten from *Zuikaku*, were prepared to sink US ships. These would be led by *Shokaku* division officer Lt Matsumura Katsuhisa, sitting as an observer in the lead Val. The main formation would approach the target at 22,000ft, escorted by 15 *Shokaku* Zero-sen, with separate formations of Zero-sen ahead and above to ward off anticipated Allied fighters.

The first aircraft to launch was a 201 Ku Zero-sen at 1010hrs, followed by Morita's 27 fighters from 204 Ku. While these formations circled Lakunai, Matsumura's 26 Vals commenced departure five minutes later from Vunakanau. Finally, Notomi's 40 Zero-sen commenced their departure at 1030hrs and set climb for the one-and-a-half-hour flight to target. At exactly midday, from the vantage of 22,000ft, the American ships came into sight.

As usual, a roster of dawn-to-dusk Allied fighter CAP had been scheduled to cover the unloading ships which had anchored offshore at 0852hrs, while offshore destroyers acted as guardians in a screen formation. The CAP was made up of an eclectic assortment of units and aircraft types, including Hellcats, Corsairs, P-40s, and P-38s operating with the USMC, USN, USAAF, and RNZAF. The first to arrive overhead that morning were eight Segi-based VF-40 Hellcats, which loitered overhead Torokina then departed with nil contact. Neither did follow-on Corsairs from VMF-215, VF-17, VMF-211, or the P-40s from the RNZAF fight the Japanese. However, there had already been an Allied casualty; that morning a band of low cloud lay between Munda and the ships. Several formations en route to Torokina diverted to fly around it, costing the life of 70th Fighter Squadron pilot Lt Herbert Schafer, whose P-40M disappeared when he failed to emerge from thick cloud.

First to intercept the advance Zero-sen formation were eight 339th Fighter Squadron P-38s led by Major Henry Lawrence. When they dove toward the Zero-sen at 1205hrs, they formed into a Lufbery circle, a giveaway that these were fighters from the land-based units 201 Ku and 204 Ku. This defensive maneuver emanates from World War I and was effective in countering the less agile P-38s. From aboard destroyer USS *Wadsworth*, the flight controller told Lawrence that a separate formation, this one including dive-bombers, was now

Commander of VF-17, Lt-Cdr John Blackburn, lands aboard USS *Bunker Hill* on November 11 to refuel while conducting CAP for the Essex Group carriers whose air contingent were away striking Rabaul. He led 23 Munda-based VF-17 Corsairs (one abort) from F4U-1A BuNo 17649 Squadron #1 named "BIG HOG."

threatening the ships offshore the beachhead. USS *Conway* also tasked a combined formation of six 44th and 70th Fighter Squadron P-40s led by Captain John Voss in the area to come to the defense of the ships and beachhead. Meanwhile, Barakoma-based VMF-212 Corsairs intercepted the incoming Vals and Zero-sen at 18,000ft, just before the Vals started their dive to target. The land-based units now broke off their Lufbery and also reached the main grouping gathering over the beachhead about 15 minutes later. This then hastily turned into a wild and spreading dogfight.

The Vals made dive-bombing attacks which lasted around 20 minutes, with the first ship-mounted AA opening fire at 1205hrs, leading its fire into a formation of Vals at 12,000ft. Six minutes later, USS *President Jackson* was hit by a bomb which failed to explode. It ricocheted off the port king-post then impacted the coaming on the #4 hold. It was later picked up and thrown off the ship by sailors after causing nothing more than a few superstructure dents. At 1225hrs USS *Hopkins* shot down a Val, a precursor to numerous claims made against Vals, in particular by USS *President Adams*, USS *Hopkins*, and USS *Fuller*. This last ship came worst off when it was damaged by two direct hits and one near-miss, killing six sailors and wounding 18.

D3A2 Vals from *Zuikaku* attacking ships and supplies just offshore Torokina on November 8

Just after midday on November 8, 26 D3A2 Vals from *Zuikaku* and *Shokaku* dive-bombed ships offshore the beachhead at Torokina. Ten *Zuikaku* Vals were led by pilot FPO1c Yoshitaka Ogashiwa, one of ten dive-bombers shot down during the attack, four from *Zuikaku* and six from *Shokaku*. Attack transport USS *President Adams* (APA-19) had just completed unloading US 37th Division and 1st Marine Amphibious Corps troops offshore Torokina. It was attacked by *Zuikaku* Val dive-bombers just after midday after becoming underway. Its 20mm AA weapons had insufficient range to register effective hits against the Vals until they were in the final moments of attack. The Vals scored hits against two transports, with near misses to another and a nearby destroyer, with USS *President Adams* remaining unscathed. The illustration shows a Val from behind, with its bomb just released. USS *President Adams* is just below with the coast nearby.

Lightning pilot Captain Bill Harris poses with 339th Fighter Squadron #5 at Guadalcanal, an early olive drab P-38J-5. Harris was promoted to captain shortly before Operation *Ro-Go* and flew in several CAP missions. He later became commander of the 18th Fighter Group in the Philippines.

Meanwhile, as the above aerial battle continued apace, a curious incident occurred when VMF-212 Corsair pilot Captain Wilbur Free had five of his six guns jam when he attacked a Val from the rear. Nonetheless, he was certain he killed its gunner, later reporting it was "last seen scooting west at an altitude of about 25ft." Exaggerated claims dominate the Allied version of this battle; however, the facts are that seven *Shokaku* Vals were lost, an eighth force-landed on the way home, and one unidentified crew member was later rescued. Four *Zuikaku* Vals were shot down, with the fifth written off after it returned to Vunakanau, carrying its dead gunner, possibly Free's victim as outlined above. All surviving carrier aircraft had returned to Rabaul by 1325hrs, with the last land-based aircraft to return a 201 Ku Zero-sen, landing at 1400hrs.

Now we address the number of Zero-sen lost, again wildly overstated in all Western post-war accounts. Both *Zuiho* and *Shokaku* lost one pilot each, respectively being FPO1c Muraoka Nobutaka and a pilot who cannot be identified due to the eccentric handwriting of the *Shokaku* operations clerk. Leading Airman Hida Ebisu was the only Zero-sen pilot lost with 201 Ku, and 204 Ku lost no fighters except one was later junked at Lakunai flown by Leading Airman Yamakawa Kiyoshi. Although his badly shot-up Zero-sen never flew again, Yamakawa got away with light injuries and was soon back in the air. Thus, we can account for three Zero-sen losses. The fourth, however, eclipsed all others.

In the confusion of battle, prominent *Zuikaku* division officer and strike commander Lt Notomi Kenjiro disappeared, a victim to an unidentified American fighter. Thus far Notomi had been the key operations officer of Operation *Ro-Go*. His talent and leadership were priceless commodities for units bereft of such qualities at this late stage of the South Seas campaign. An inexperienced and green cadre of young carrier pilots looked to him for inspiration and guidance throughout the operation.

In the 40-minute fight which spread from Torokina to Buka Passage from between 12,000 to 22,000ft, some focus is justified to examine claims versus actual losses. Japanese debits of four Zero-sen and 11 Vals bring total Japanese losses to 15 aircraft. It is clear from the ship's meticulous and specific AA reports that these gunners dispatched at least seven Vals, leaving eight aircraft shot down by US fighters. However, the 44th and 70th Fighter Squadron P-40s made six definite claims; the 339th Lightnings claimed eight (whose cadre included one 12th Fighter Squadron pilot), VMF-212 claimed three Vals, and VF-33 Hellcats claimed six definites. Behind this total claim of 23 "definites" against eight actually shot down lies a more ominous consideration, for the Americans in fact lost six fighters against the Japanese four. To be fair, the Americans were outnumbered. However, the real losses tell a different story to the one more commonly presented in Western histories.

A VMF-212 Corsair flown by 1/Lt Edward Brown went missing, likely shot down and crashed in the sea south of Torokina, as did a VF-33 Hellcat flown by Ens M. E. Patterson.

Another VF-33 Hellcat ditched in shallow water near Torokina River; its pilot Lt (jg) J. J. Kinsella, stood on the wing to attract the attention of a nearby US craft, which soon rescued him. He subsequently claimed three of VF-33's six kills. P-38 pilot Lt Carl Squires was shot down and killed by Zero-sen around 1215hrs, and similarly, 44th Fighter Squadron P-40M pilot Lt John Dollen was also shot down, but he too was soon rescued. Lt John Voss broadcast he was going to try to ditch his 44th Fighter Squadron fighter near Mono Island where there were friendly troops. However, he lost control of his new P-40M when it stalled at low altitude, driving into the waters between Mono and Stirling Islands and exploding. The USN lost one more airframe when VF-33 pilot Lt (jg) J. W. Rankin landed his badly shot-up F6F at Barakoma. A badly wounded Rankin had to be lifted from the cockpit; he later recounted from his hospital bed how he shot down one Val and killed the gunner from a second.

The final act of aerial defiance for this day played out over the beachhead into the early hours of November 9 when a pair of 938 Ku Jakes departed Buka half an hour apart, commencing at 2200hrs. They dropped 60kg (132lb) bombs into the beachhead from 2305hrs to 0110hrs, impeded by atrocious weather. In the face of the same conditions, the second diverted to the Shortlands, where it landed at 0220hrs, returning to Buka early next morning.

Night attack against the cruisers – November 8–9

As demonstrated to date, ongoing reports of substantive shipping movements ensured constant Japanese reconnaissance of Bougainville's waters. Widespread USN shipping movement was ubiquitous, a result of both efforts to protect the landing and to ensure ongoing logistics supply, including safeguarding Mono Island. At 1630hrs Vunakanau's communications center received a report from a *Zuikaku* Judy flown by WO Yoshikawa Takeshi of three battleships attended by numerous ships sailing between the Treasury Islands and Bougainville. This was indeed the case; Yoshikawa had found the three cruisers of Cruiser Division 13, comprising USS *Birmingham*, *Santa Fe*, and *Mobile*, accompanied by destroyers USS *Harrison*, *John Rodgers*, *McKee*, and *Murray*.

This flotilla was covering the Torokina landing area and late afternoon found it patrolling northwest of the Treasury Islands. After the sun set at 1815hrs, the moon was sporadically cloaked behind cloud and squalls scoured the sea. Cruiser USS *Birmingham* was equipped with the latest FD radar purpose-designed to direct antiaircraft guns. The FD radar sets worked well, and detected approaching distant aircraft with relative ease. The cruisers and destroyers were also equipped with a range of 5-inch, 40mm, and 20mm antiaircraft weapons. Combined with FD radar, it was inevitable that the forthcoming hours would prove costly for the Japanese, this time to the tune of four Kates and eight Bettys.

Fixated again on attacking yet another shipping threat as reported by Yoshikawa, Rabaul planned an all-out strike, this time incorporating torpedo-equipped Bettys of 702 Ku and 751 Ku. Rabaul's first task was to confirm the flotilla's size and position, so to initiate matters it launched four Kates (two *Shokaku*, two *Zuikaku*) at 1700hrs. Half an hour later nine more Kates (four *Zuikaku*, five *Shokaku*) departed, led by *Shokaku* division officer and observer Lt Ono Hiroji, who rode in the lead aircraft. For reasons best

The central IJN communications center located close to Vunakanau. All radio communications, including those from aircraft and observation posts, came through this center. Important messages were relayed immediately to relevant headquarters by telephone.

known to the planners, these Kates toted 60kg (132lb) bombs instead of torpedoes. From 1913hrs, these Kates made sporadic low-level attack runs for 13 minutes against two cruisers and several destroyers. At 1917hrs, cruiser USS *Birmingham* was hit by a 60kg bomb, which killed one sailor and blew another overboard. Two minutes later, the wreckage of two brightly burning aircraft could be seen on the port quarter, while to starboard green and red flares bobbed on the ocean surface. While they were a considerable distance, the flares ominously surrounded the flotilla. At 1942hrs, another Kate made another run, this time against a destroyer; however, concentrated gunfire saw the attack bomber explode as it passed overhead and then disintegrated into the ocean. In similar manner, four *Shokaku* Kates were destroyed in the darkness. The surviving nine of 13 returned to Vunakanau at 2112hrs.

Meanwhile, all USN gunnery continued to be guided by FD radar in the pitch darkness. Visual sightings had been fleeting, only possible when attackers closed to 2,000yds or less. Accordingly, it is difficult to align specific crews with losses, particularly for the next two phases of attack by a dozen torpedo-equipped Bettys. These two stages were planned by 702 Ku pilot Lt (jg) Sato Yutaka, and 751 Ku pilot Lt Nozaka Michio. First away at 1714hrs were six 751 Ku Bettys led by Nozaka, followed five minutes later by a 702 Ku pair, then the main 702 Ku force of six Bettys led by Sato. These 14 land-attack bombers comprised the first phase of the evening's activities, with a separate smaller phase to follow in the early hours of next morning.

Most of this first Betty assault, despite their persistence, were either gunned down or dissuaded from pressing accurate attacks. The six 751 Ku Bettys made individual runs commencing at 1910hrs for 15 minutes, with three shot down. Then the six 702 Ku Bettys did the same, also losing three. This included an attack at 1958hrs, in which a Betty dropped green flares before being shot down at a range of 14,000yds. It burst into flames then struck water 2,000yds distant from the cruisers. At the end of this first phase lookouts aboard USS *Birmingham* counted the surrounding wreckage of eight aircraft burning on the water. The last 702 Ku survivor returned to Vunakanau at 2150hrs; however, these Bettys returned without mission leader Lt (jg) Sato Yutaka, and two more commanded by WO Miho Kunimi and WO Ogawa Harakyo.

751 Ku Betty tail code 51-352 at Vunakanau during Operation *Ro-Go*.

A Betty departs Vunakanau. Note the bomb bay has no door, removed when carrying either bombs or torpedoes.

The second phase of the attack was made by four 751 Ku Bettys which departed Vunakanau at 2120hrs. Their modus operandi saw them make similarly unsuccessful torpedo attacks between 2330hrs and 0417hrs, losing two more Bettys. A highlight of this phase occurred at 0100hrs, when a Betty dived out of cloud toward cruiser USS *Mobile*. After dropping its torpedo, which missed, it crashed into the ocean after passing overhead. Seconds later, another Betty appeared from exactly the opposite direction. It too was hit by ships' gunfire, but it burned brightly as it continued straight and level for nearly half a minute before finally exploding on the ocean surface. These Bettys, like their predecessors, also dropped flares around the flotilla. From 0103hrs to 0240hrs, USS *Birmingham*'s 5-inch battery engaged nine separate targets under full FD radar control. The two surviving 751 Ku Bettys arrived back at Vunakanau at 0500hrs. Five 751 Ku Betty crews were lost to both attack phases, including mission leader Lt Nozaka Michio and four more flown or commanded by WO Arae Toshio, WO Marugo Shigeru, FCPO Takeda Akeo, and Lt (jg) Kaneda Yoshikazu.

That night, 938 Ku officer Ens Ohane Otoji coordinated two pairs of reconnaissance Jakes, each from 938 Ku and 958 Ku, to reconnoiter the Treasury Islands. The first 938 Ku Jake launched from Buka between squalls at 1905hrs with Ohane as observer; the second followed ten minutes later. Ohane found 15 ships offshore Mono Island, but the weather was so bad his Jake diverted to the Shortlands at 2330hrs, where it overnighted before returning to Buka next morning. The second floatplane from this pair turned back in the face of a wall of rain and was taxiing back in Buka's harbor an hour later. The second 958 Ku pair waited for the weather to improve before departing at exactly midnight, and from 0140hrs to 0340hrs they wandered over the same ships being targeted by the torpedo Bettys, counting about 20 ships in two groups.

Next morning Rabaul staff officers struggled to make sufficient sense of the returnee's claims to know whether the Kates and Bettys had attacked the same target. Confronted by the substantive ship-count as reported by the Jakes, they concurred two separate concentrations of ships must have been attacked. They then distilled the hysterical claims of numbers of ships sunk down to "considerable results." In fact, not one US ship had been sunk.

Aviators in raft – November 9

The final chapter of this terrible night for the Japanese played out with a sobering episode the following afternoon. One of the Bettys shot down ditched cleanly, and its crew took to the dull red rescue dinghy stored behind every Betty's dorsal gun position. Hoping to be collected by a Japanese vessel, or perhaps reach Japanese-occupied territory, they instead were approached the following afternoon at 1545hrs by USS *Spence*. They had drifted thus far southeast in the vicinity of Simbo Island. Unhappy events as they now unfolded were logged by the destroyer as follows:

> On closing several bodies were noted in float as it passed close aboard down starboard side. Seven men who had been feigning death sat up and started talking in Japanese. One, apparently an officer and pilot, broke out a 7.7mm machine gun (evidently a free gun salvaged from plane). Each man in succession placed the muzzle of the gun in his mouth and the officer fired a round, blowing the back of the man's head out. The first to be killed showed great reluctance to be included in the suicide pact. One man held him while another wielded the machine gun. All of the bodies toppled over the side and sank, followed closely by several sharks. The officer, alone on the raft, gave a short farewell speech or harangue to the Commanding Officer on the bridge then shot himself. Total time was only about five minutes. Grapnels were made fast and the raft hoisted aboard. All bodies were lost before they could be caught by grapnels.

The Beaufort push – November 8–9

Subsequent to the conventional results of the November 5 Beaufort mission, RAAF Air Commodore "Joe" Hewitt was now anticipating a more substantive Beaufort torpedo strike. Determined to showcase a RAAF success, several participating Beauforts had been grounded in the lead-up period to ensure their serviceability. Hewitt had a good grasp of the challenges his crews faced. A former naval officer and Fleet Air Arm pilot, a much-invested Hewitt had so far involved himself closely in the operational planning. This entailed a dozen No. 8 Squadron Beaufort torpedo-equipped bombers headed for Simpson harbour, while other Beauforts would bomb Rapopo and Vunakanau to create a diversion.

Ground crew run into underground concrete air-raid shelter #2 at Rapopo airfield. These shelters could house up to 100 personnel.

Late that afternoon Beaufort A9-255 was dispatched to conduct a preliminary reconnaissance, returning in haste when it was pursued by three ship-borne Jakes near the harbor at 2035hrs. Upon return to Kiriwina the Beaufort's observer reported heavy rain in the area; however, he was also adamant that in anticipation of a torpedo attack, the ships in the harbor had grouped their ships defensively to maximize an antiaircraft barrage. This was not the case; the IJN ships were anchored in their usual positions as dictated by IJN doctrine.

The observer's adamancy agitated the waiting crews at Kiriwina. In a subsequent conference held outdoors the operations hut, a flight commander approached Hewitt, exclaiming that the "show was off." Hewitt, faced with an unexpected command crisis, now tried to guide morale back on track, but tempers were laid threadbare during ensuing heated discussion held over a spread map of the Rabaul area, draped over a jeep bonnet. While the squadron commanders debated matters, the Beaufort crews waited uneasily in the background for word to go. Hewitt was determined to see the carefully planned mission proceed but was reluctant to over-rule the commander of the mission. The future role of the Beaufort in RAAF service was on the line, and the window of launch opportunity was fast running out. In order to defuse the situation, Hewitt suggested a compromise that three aircraft go instead of the full complement of 12 as originally planned. He asked for volunteers, hoping all 12 crews would step forward. This did not happen, and instead only three Beauforts departed together at 1230hrs in the early hours of November 9 loaded with Mk 12 torpedoes.

The three negotiated thunderstorms en route but the weather cleared as they approached Rabaul low, around 100ft, in "V" formation, then formed into a queue through the narrow neck of land which leads from Talili Bay into the harbor. They flew though a barrage of antiaircraft fire at 0240hrs but their attack was unsuccessful. Two Beauforts returned to

A RAAF Beaufort taxies out at Kiriwina for another night mission over Rabaul in late 1943.

Kiriwina just before dawn broke. The third never returned; Squadron Leader Owen Price and his crew had been blasted from the sky, killing all three crew.

November 10

By early evening, more reasonable weather was in the offing, so Rabaul decided again to strike the merchantmen offshore Torokina beachhead, along with shore positions recently established by the US invaders. The task this time was assigned to *Zuikaku* division officer Lt Miyao Usuru. He dispatched three Kates on a preliminary search mission which left at 1900hrs. The trio carried no ordnance but had long-range tanks attached, and after searching the area they returned at midnight. They reported confirmation that several smaller vessels were offshore but little else. The USN was in the process of establishing a PT base on Puruata Island, just offshore the beachhead, and the Kates had seen recently arrived patrol boats roaming the area.

A strike force of 14 Kates divided into two groups was assembled, drawn from *Zuiho*, *Shokaku*, and *Zuikaku*. These were led by Miyao himself who flew the first Kate; at 1950hrs, the first formation of eight Kates departed toting 60kg (132lb) bombs, followed 20 minutes later by a second group of six carrying torpedoes. The results for the Japanese were derisory; at 2215hrs, an attacking flight of three was caught in searchlights. They launched their torpedoes at the lights, unclear whether they were ship- or shore-based. In the event they were the latter, and all torpedoes pointlessly ran aground. In the next half hour during multiple attacks, several bombs fell into the Puruata Island boat pool, killing two sailors and wounding 13. At 2254hrs, one Kate released its torpedo against patrol boat *PT-61*, but a tight turn by the skipper successfully and easily evaded the weapon. *PT-319* put a sustained burst of machine-gun fire into the belly of another Kate as it passed overhead. This Kate, hit by gunfire, descended inland and crashed. Its wreckage was located one mile inland from the beach the next day. The base mine unit removed the warhead from the torpedo which still lay in the wreckage. They then removed and buried the burned corpses of the unidentified three aircrew.

Nine surviving Kates from this mission returned to Vunakanau at 0200hrs, but five had been lost of the 14 dispatched. Mission leader Lt Miyao Usuru went MIA, as did a second *Zuikaku* Kate. *Shokaku* pilot FPO1c Sato Yasuhiko was fished out of Empress Augusta Bay by a destroyer the next morning, claiming he had ditched due to an engine failure. This was true, although undoubtedly the "engine failure" was combat-induced. He claimed his other two crew were lost, along with tail code A1-2-303, when it sank. However, although some parts of his story do not add up, Sato did give his real name and correct rank, confirmed from the *Shokaku* operations sheet, and he spent the rest of the war as a POW in New Caledonia. The fate of the third missing *Shokaku* Kate lost is opaque; it was listed as having ditched although the crew's ultimate fate is unknown. Next morning at 0625hrs, patrol boat *PT-319* pulled an unconscious Kate crew member from the water. While he was being stripped to give him dry clothing, he came to, then jumped overboard pleading to be shot. All efforts to haul him back aboard failed, so the patrol boat crew obliged his wishes. *PT-171* approached another unidentified Kate crewmember in the water who stabbed himself several times as they neared. He was brought aboard, stripped, then restrained, although his ultimate fate is unclear.

Away from the Kate mission, that evening 938 Ku officer Lt (jg) Masaki Yukio flew as an observer in a Jake from Buka. The floatplane at first headed for the seas south of Mono, where at 2345hrs ten USN ships materialized into view before Masaki headed home via the Torokina beachhead; overhead at 0150hrs he reported one merchantman on fire. It is unclear what Masaki had seen; however, the sighting was sufficient for Rabaul staff officers to record it as a successful sinking from the Kate mission, which was not the case.

Meanwhile, inland from the beachhead, Japanese soldiers attacked against the forwardmost American outpost pushing toward Piva village. The attack was repulsed with heavy US

casualties, but by the evening of November 10 Piva had been occupied without opposition. Now firmly in US hands, construction of the first airfield would commence the next morning.

Rabaul's night skies

Although not directly part of Operation *Ro-Go*, the efforts of 251 Ku need to be addressed in the period. The night defenders of Rabaul, this was a fighter unit which had completely changed its stripes. Reincarnated back in Japan from the decimated Tainan Ku, 251 Ku had at first reappeared in Rabaul in May 1943 with Model 22 Zero-sen.

The unit's fate gives context to the pressures facing the Japanese during Operation *Ro-Go*. Back on June 30, 1943, alongside other units opposing the American landings at Rendova, substantive aerial combat had unfolded. Of the two dozen 251 Ku Zero-sen which flew the mission, eight had been shot down or went missing, two pilots badly wounded, one Zero-sen destroyed on crash-landing, and six more had incurred airframe damage. This was secondary to the main blow, being that 251 Ku's leadership had been eradicated in one fell swoop; those lost included *buntaicho* Lt Mukai Ichiro, and two *chutaicho*, Lts Hashimoto Mitsuteru and O'ono Takeyoshi. Withdrawn to Rabaul, its much-deployed Zero-sen continued operations in the Solomons until September 1, 1943, when the unit was reclassified as a night-fighter unit. Allocated the J1N1-S twin-engine Irving, on September 1, 1943, Commander Kusumoto Ikuto was appointed as the unit's commander to implement the unit's new role. This was a marked change for Kusumoto, who had previously served as *hikocho* of the Takao and Kanoya bomber groups, followed by his most recent appointment as staff officer with the 2nd Fleet.

Administrative buildings for an AA unit headquartered near Vunakanau. The white circle indicates a Shinto shrine, and nearby several personnel are looking upwards at the low-level USAAF B-25 which has taken them by surprise. Two 40mm and one 20mm sunken gun pits can be seen in the photo.

VF-18 Hellcats about to launch from USS *Bunker Hill* on November 11.

Although officially allocated two dozen night-fighters, by the time of Operation *Ro-Go*, 251 Ku struggled to maintain eight airworthy J1N1-S on Lakunai's flightline. Chief supply officer Lt Wada Masa'aki labored to obtain ample spares for the thoroughbred twins, and resultant airframe damage from night combat often grounded aircraft. By the time of Operation *Ro-Go*, 251 Ku's main role had thus turned to defending Rabaul's skies; however, it was mostly operating single-aircraft missions in reaction to reports of incoming bombers in order to conserve resources.

Its most experienced observer in late 1943 was FCPO O'onuma Masatake, who regularly flew the night missions. Single sorties were flown most nights, from the commencement of Operation *Ro-Go* until the evening of November 9–10, when four Irvings were airborne over Rabaul. They patrolled between 2235hrs and 0720hrs, and the following evening of November 10–11 conducted five sorties to do the same. Two Irvings separately exchanged gunfire at 2125hrs and at 0430hrs the next morning with USN PB4Y-1 Liberators. Conducting snooping missions from Guadalcanal, these Liberators appeared again the following evening of November 11–12. As was the wont of the weather during Operation *Ro-Go*, a resultant six separate sorties saw two night-fighters return to Rabaul early because of foul weather. Thus we can see that while Rabaul enjoyed the advantage of advanced-technology aircraft such as the J1N1-S, it had insufficient numbers to make a difference.

The November 11 Rabaul strike

Now we turn to the two pivotal and concluding battles of Operation *Ro-Go*, when a follow-on USN Rabaul carrier strike was returned by a Japanese counterstrike. For the Japanese this came at ruinous cost. To understand how the situation unfolded, we return to when Admiral Chester Nimitz authorized use of a second carrier task force by Admiral William "Bull" Halsey to strike Rabaul for a second time. As was the case previously with the November 5 strike, this strike set for November 11 had to be organized at short notice. The carriers were on temporary loan until November 14, after which they were earmarked for the Central Pacific to support the Gilbert Islands invasion.

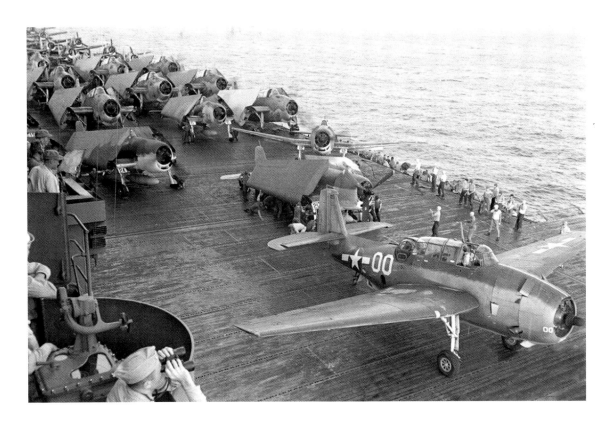

The dispatched task force TG50.3, termed "The Essex Group," comprised three carriers: two Essex-class USS *Essex* and USS *Bunker Hill*, and light carrier USS *Independence*, accompanied by a screen of nine destroyers, *Chauncy, Kidd, Bullard, McKee, Murray, Edwards, Sterrett, Wilson,* and *Stack*. Memorably, the strike marked the combat debut of the Helldiver, whose introduction to service had been problematic. Commanded by Rear Admiral Alfred Montgomery, this carrier task force would launch to the west of Empress Augusta Bay, only 138 nautical miles from Rabaul.

This close proximity required constant CAP, provided by land-based squadrons; 23 Munda-based VF-17 Corsairs (one abort) commanded by Lt-Cdr John Blackburn. These Corsairs would be refueled aboard *Bunker Hill* during the strike coordinated by USS *Essex*'s flight director. Prior to departing Munda engineers reattached the Corsairs' tail hooks. USS *Bunker Hill* had been the carrier upon which VF-17 had made their shakedown cruise in the Caribbean. This exceptional event marked the first carrier-based combat sortie for the Corsair, contradicting the popular narrative that the British achieved this goal.

This was a two-pronged attack; separately, Admiral Forrest Sherman's TF38 with carriers *Princeton* and *Saratoga* would launch directly east of Buka, 197 nautical miles distant from Rabaul. The initial weather forecast was that Rabaul was covered in heavy cloud; when and if it would dissipate was anyone's guess. TF38 enjoyed the protection of destroyers *San Juan, San Diego, Grayson, Woodworth, Buchanan, Lansdowne, Lardner,* and *Farenholt*. Eleven VF-33 Hellcats led by Lt J. C. Kelly based at Segi Point would provide CAP for these two carriers while the strike force was away. At 0742hrs the first of these Hellcats landed on USS *Saratoga* to be refueled.

In the end one strike was an hour late, and the other half an hour early, resulting in an unplanned almost-simultaneous attack. *Saratoga* completed its launches from 0520hrs to 0547hrs with 36 Hellcats, 23 SBDs, and 17 TBFs. The attack was coordinated by USN Commander Henry Caldwell from his TBF uniquely numbered #00, escorted by VF-12

Commander Henry Caldwell peers behind from the cockpit of his TBF aboard USS *Saratoga* on November 11, with #00 being reserved for the commander of VT-12 who also acted as CAG-12 mission leader. Lined up behind are VF-12 F6F Hellcats #21 and 24, which will escort him over Rabaul.

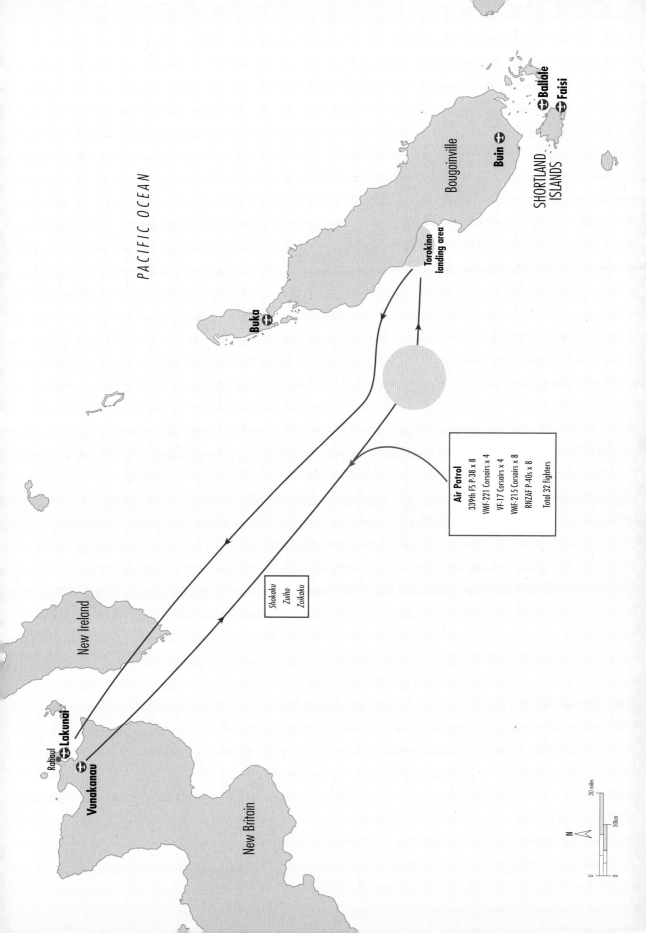

PACIFIC OCEAN

Ballale
Faisi

SHORTLAND
ISLANDS

Buin

Bougainville

Torokina
landing area

Buka

Air Patrol

339th FS P-38 x 8
VMF-221 Corsairs x 4
VF-17 Corsairs x 4
VMF-215 Corsairs x 8
RNZAF P-40s x 8

Total 32 fighters

New Ireland

Shokaku
Zuiho
Zuikaku

Lakunai
Rabaul
Vunakanau

New Britain

N

0   30 miles
0   30km

Hellcats #21 and 24. *Princeton* launched 22 Hellcats and nine TBFs. *Essex* launched its Air Group 9, starting at 0645hrs with 18 VT-9 TBFs (plus one more for group commander, Commander Paul Emrick), 28 VB-9 SBD-5s, and 29 VF-9 Hellcats. *Bunker Hill* launched 27 VF-18 Hellcats, 23 VB-17 Helldivers, and 19 VT-17 TBFs, including the CAG-18 commander's aircraft. *Independence* launched nine VC-22 TBFs, eight VF-22 Hellcats, and eight more from VF-6. In terms of numbers this was an impressive strike; these five carriers launched a total inventory of 274 aircraft: 70 TBF Avengers, 130 F6F Hellcats, 51 SBDs, and 23 SB2C Helldivers.

VB-17 Helldivers return to USS *Bunker Hill* for a left-hand circuit following the November 11 strike, the first combat mission for the type in World War II.

Target Rabaul – again

Since November 5 all IJN heavy cruisers had left Rabaul except *Maya*, which was undergoing engine repairs to enable it to return to Japan. Thus, although maritime targets at Rabaul were confined to light cruisers, destroyers, and auxiliary vessels, there was a sufficient number on hand to justify a strike. Also in American favor was the consideration that there would be fewer Japanese aircraft to oppose the Americans. This was due to substantive Japanese losses in the past week; nonetheless, these had been considerably over-estimated by the Americans.

As usual the weather conditions continued to disrupt the plans of both sides. A B-24 raid planned against Rabaul from Guadalcanal the same day was turned back by weather.

An explosion is seen off the port stern of USS *Bunker Hill* on November 11, caused by a near-miss from a 250kg bomb delivered by a Val. The TBFs on deck are assigned to VT-17. Strike leader Lt Sato Masao was lost in his Zero-sen on this mission.

The first strike found *Saratoga* and *Princeton*'s aircraft negotiating a littoral of rain squalls in their efforts to find shipping targets. These aircraft attacked a light cruiser and four destroyers on their only strike, inflicting only minor damage. Weather cancelled a second strike, but these two carriers withdrew undetected, thus evading Japanese retribution. Around the carriers the day remained cloudy throughout with scattered showers, visibility between 12 and 30 miles, and an east wind blowing an unyielding 11 knots. Flying conditions in *Saratoga*'s log are described as "average."

The Americans hoped they would not be spotted, but it was hard to see how the Essex task force in particular could escape detection. Their launch area lay square in the search area being methodically patrolled around the clock by both 938 Ku and 958 Ku Jakes operating from Buka. Throughout late evening of November 10, the lights burned bright over large-scale charts laid over a wooden desk inside the former Australian colonial building occupied by Admiral Kusaka's staff officers. One report in particular received at 2345hrs that evening was the most alarming; it referenced two aircraft carriers bearing 203 degrees from Mono Island at a distance of 26 nautical miles. Underlining its importance was the descriptor that ten escorting vessels surrounded the two carriers in circular arrangement. Furthermore, the Jake responsible for the report was commanded by Lt (jg) Masaki Yukio, an officer and experienced observer. The sighting was confirmed at 0350hrs the next morning by another

Jake, this time from a 958 Ku crew with pilot Leading Airman Sugiki Yoshikazu, who returned to Buka at 0440hrs. More Jake patrols followed on with similar sightings.

With the Japanese now laser-focused on a carrier group they had found offshore Torokina, it was not surprising they did not find TF38 – centered around carriers *Saratoga* and *Princeton* – as it was off their beaten reconnaissance path. Shouting woke up aircrew all over Rabaul as a dawn strike against the carriers was ordered. The strike was to be led by *Zuiho* division officer and pilot Lt Sato Masao, appointed as the best replacement for *Zuikaku* division officer and strike commander Lt Notomi Kenjiro, lost only three days before. Sato rested on solid combat credentials; inter alia he had flown among the *Zuikaku* fighters which strafed Kaneohe at Pearl Harbor. He had subsequently seen much action as a division officer aboard *Kaga* in May–June 1942, and had been appointed to his current position only five months previously.

Nonetheless, Japanese impatience to get airborne was tempered by thick cloud which hung over Rabaul and refused to move. Thus, the dawn attack was deferred, with launch delayed several hours in the hope the cloud would dissipate. Finally, just when the decision was "go," the USN carrier planes arrived. To better understand the weather conditions which governed this attack we turn to a post-strike USS *Saratoga* précis which reads, "The lack of more suitable targets is deplored. The attack had to be executed immediately or the opportunity would have been lost as the only visible targets were underway at high speed racing for the cover of a large squall over Praed Point."

All Zero-sen units scrambled at exactly 0900hrs to meet the Americans, placing 107 Zero-sen in the air, and commencing first contact ten minutes later. These comprised a dozen fighters each from *Zuiho* and *Zuikaku*, 15 from *Shokaku*, 19 from 201 Ku, 25 from 253 Ku, and two dozen from 204 Ku.

Losses to ensue were three *Zuiho* Zero-sen, including Ens Yamada Shoichiro, two from 201 Ku, two from 253 Ku, including Leading Airman Shibayama Sekizen, and one 204 Ku Zero-sen, with another 204 Ku pilot hospitalized with serious injuries. Despite generous USN claims, Japanese losses were confined to eight Zero-sen, less than the USN losses. Perhaps the most unlucky Zero-sen pilot was Shibayama, who commenced the morning as a non-combatant in order to ferry a Model 52 Zero-sen to Truk. Just after departing Tobera he experienced engine trouble. Just when he was trying to address the matter, VF-9 Hellcats unexpectedly holed his Zero-sen in the cockpit and engine, wounding Shibayama in the knee. This was likely Hellcat pilot Lt Armistead Smith, whose second claimed victory noted that his victim ditched offshore Matupi Island, the same location as Shibayama.

The attackers' losses were a mixture of combat and operational, and comprised more operational losses than anticipated, including several at launch. *Essex* lost VB-9 SBD-5 #7 shot down off Cape Gazelle by Zero-sen, then VF-9 F6F-3 #26 ditched by Ens Robert Kapp at the entrance to Simpson Harbour who remains MIA. Three VT-9 TBFs were lost: two splashed on launch and another ditched near the carrier on return. *Bunker Hill* lost two VF-18 F6Fs over Rabaul to Zero-sen, and two more ditched on return when unable to lower their gear. Two VB-17 Helldivers were lost to operational causes: one ditched on return near

VB-17 SB2C-1 Helldivers from USS *Bunker Hill* dive-bombing Rabaul on November 11, 1943

Lt-Commander James Vose leads SB2C-1 Helldivers from VB-17 which had launched from USS *Bunker Hill* on the morning of November 11. The Helldivers, flying their first combat mission of the war, arrived overhead Blanche Bay at 0910hrs at 11,000ft, with broken cloud below at around 2,000ft. They commenced dive-bombing Japanese ships anchored in the harbor between rain squalls which also pervaded the area. During these attacks, destroyer *Suzunami* took a direct bomb hit while loading torpedoes, blew up and sank killing 148 including the ship's captain, Commander Masao Kamiyama. The illustration shows Vose flying #4, over Blanche Bay about to commence dive-bombing.

A pilot and observer prepare to board a reconnaissance D4Y1-C at Lakunai. An assistant crewman carries the observer's plotting chart and flight bag while another crewman prepares the cockpit. Note the long-range fuel tank attached to a hard point underneath the left wing.

the carrier, and the other lost power on takeoff, drowning the pilot. Two VT-17 TBFs went MIA over Rabaul. *Saratoga* lost three VT-12 TBFs: Lt Stefan Nyarady was shot down by AA, taken POW, and repatriated from Japan after the war; Lt Harlan Burrus was also taken POW but was executed a few weeks later. The third TBF was blasted out of the sky by a direct AA burst. *Saratoga* lost its only F6F when its pilot parachuted safely near the carrier on return. *Independence* lost three F6Fs: Lt Bascom Gates went MIA, one ditched near the carrier on return when the pilot could not lower his gear, and another ditched near Rabaul, its pilot strafed by Zero-sen.

To add to this costly list were two VF-17 Corsairs which ditched on the way home due to fuel exhaustion, both pilots recovered. Finally, VF-33 lost one F6F when its pilot Lt John Kelley went MIA after being seen to ditch. As such the raid directly cost a total of 23 American aircraft: eight TBFs, ten Hellcats, two Helldivers, one SBD, and two Corsairs, thus incurring nearly three times the number of aircraft lost as the Japanese.

The raid nonetheless again rattled the Japanese and did considerable damage to the remaining ships in the harbor. The biggest success occurred when a *Bunker Hill* Helldiver attacked destroyer *Suzunami*. It was boarding torpedoes at the harbor mouth when a squarely planted bomb caused follow-on explosions, shattering the hull and sinking the ship. A total of 148 crew was killed, including the captain, Lt-Cdr Kamiyama Masao. A TBF-launched torpedo hit light cruiser *Agano* in the stern and another torpedo hit destroyer *Naganami* abaft the No. 3 turret, rendering the ship dead in the water. It later had to be towed back for repairs. Arguably the most under-rated achievement of the raid and costly loss to the Japanese was four supply ships sunk which had yet to be unloaded, laden with valuable materiel.

Japanese retaliation

The Japanese were well aware of the position of the three Essex Group carriers while, on the northeast side of Bougainville, TF38 with culprit carriers *Princeton* and *Saratoga* scurried away from the area at full speed. By the time the last USN aircraft had left the scene, IJN staff officers were already confirming aircraft assignments for a retaliatory strike, their third attempt to launch for the day. Over at Vunakanau, *Zuiho* division officer Lt Sato Masao briefed the Zero-sen and Kate crews on their primary objective – the USN carriers. It needs to be again underlined that patchy weather still beleaguered the region all the way to the strike area, explaining several incidents about to ensue.

At 1145hrs two reconnaissance D4Y1-C Judys were dispatched. The *Zuikaku* one reported finding 15 substantial ships at 1255hrs, but the visibility in the strike area was patchy, and after transmitting a follow-on report at 1305hrs it disappeared. The *Shokaku* Judy reported "operations normal" at 1222hrs some 70 miles from Rabaul, then it too failed to return. These IJN pilots were well trained for long-distance ocean navigation, and the loss of both aircraft speaks volumes for the extant unfavorable meteorological conditions.

At exactly midday, shortly after both Judys departed, 69 Zero-sen from various units headed off to find the carriers. These included a massive formation of 32 204 Ku Zero-sen led by Lt (jg) Morita Heitaro. The participation of this land-based unit, however, turned into a debacle. Climbing between squalls, Morita's radio failed to pick up radio transmissions updating the location of their target. As they floundered around, not knowing where they should be going, Morita and his flyers shortly returned to Lakunai, having been airborne just short of two hours. Ten minutes after Morita's formation, 15 more land-based Zero-sen took off; a dozen 201 Ku fighters led by a 204 Ku flight headed by Ens Katayama, whose first name is not entered in the dispatch log. Katayama was one of several officers seconded to 201 Ku in past weeks to address the shortage of officers 201 Ku was experiencing due to combat losses. Regardless, Katayama was soon bedeviled by the same communications problems as his comrade Morita, and he too turned his formation back for Lakunai.

The purpose of these land-based Zero-sen was to fly ahead and engage expected USN fighter opposition, thus clearing a path for the strike force. This left the Zero-sen formation comprised entirely of carrier unit fighters, whose purpose was to escort the attack force. They had launched at 1216hrs shortly after 201 Ku and 204 Ku and totaled 33 Zero-sen led by Lt Sato Masao (nine *Zuikaku*, 15 *Shokaku*, and nine *Zuiho*). These fighters escorted an attack force which had launched shortly after the Zero-sen and comprised 23 Vals (seven *Zuikaku* and 16 *Shokaku*), and 14 Kates (five each from *Zuikaku* and *Shokaku*, with four more from *Zuiho*). Within minutes of departure, six Vals (three each from *Shokaku* and *Zuikaku*) returned to base with engine problems, leaving 17 Vals headed for the carriers. This depleted force of Vals was bolstered somewhat by an additional four 501 Ku Judy dive-bombers led by observer FCPO Morita Itsuo.

By 1342hrs the combined formation of 68 aircraft was cruising at 22,000ft; however, USN radar first detected an incoming hostile force at 1313hrs, a good half an hour prior when it was still 118 nautical miles distant. In the interim, the three carriers of the the Essex Group had been preparing a second strike against Rabaul, immediately cancelled when the incoming Japanese were detected. The carriers were sailing 2,000yds apart, encircled by destroyers forming a wide protective screen.

At 1343hrs the first USN fighters intercepted the incoming belligerents, some 40 miles distant from the carriers. Sixteen VT-9 TBFs, which had already launched from USS *Essex* for the cancelled second strike against Rabaul, joined USN fighters in resisting the attack, producing this caustic quote: "It is not Squadron doctrine to act as fighters in attempting to drive off attacking dive-bombers and torpedo planes. However under certain conditions it may be necessary."

Over the next half an hour there was persistent, widespread, and fierce fighting, with the main Japanese attack against the carriers occurring from 1358hrs to 1442hrs. The Vals approached first and scored near-misses against all three carriers. At 1408hrs, a complete *chutai* of nine Vals tried to bomb USS *Bunker Hill*; then, from 1404hrs to 1420hrs several Kates made individual regular low-level passes from astern, but most were destroyed by AA before they reached the ships. At 1442hrs, the final run was made by a substantive group of Kates. When it was over there had been negligible damage to the USN ships. Although the Japanese launched at least eight torpedoes at the carriers, all had missed. These torpedo

Bullet holes and shattered Perspex can be seen on VT-9 TBF #9 BuNo 47656 after the November 11 raid aboard USS *Essex*. An engineer is removing the damaged gun sight for repairs.

attacks commenced at long distance from low altitude, making them easy targets. Although not one Val had placed a bomb on the carriers, this fight had been closer to peril than might have been, certainly the opinion of those aboard USS *Essex*: ". . . all carrier decks – spotted with numerous bomb-loaded planes – were only narrowly missed. There is rather a close margin, in these affairs, between victory and disaster."

The Japanese summary concludes "excellent results but heavy losses." This glib précis, however, belittles the biggest air power calamity the Japanese had suffered in the theater to date. The Japanese lost every attacking Kate and every Val, shot down by either USN fighters or flak. Two of the four Judys were also shot down, claimed by VF-9 and VF-17 and misidentified as Tonys. Only two Zero-sen were lost, but critically one was strike leader Lt Sato Masao, who like his predecessor Lt Notomi Kenjiro, had been shot down leading a critical mission. The other Zero-sen pilot lost was *Shokaku*'s WO Sato Hitoshi. The 33 survivors returned to Rabaul from 1500hrs to 1530hrs. In exchange the US Navy had lost only four aircraft. Two Hellcats were shot down by Zero-sen, and patrolling VB-17 Helldiver #28 disappeared, it too likely shot down by absconding Japanese. One Avenger was destroyed in an operational accident. Elaborate claims were made by both sides, but especially by the Japanese, who claimed to have sunk a cruiser, damaged two aircraft carriers, and set afire three other warships, once again making Operation *Ro-Go* an exercise in fiction.

The Bettys attack

With the carriers still lurking offshore, three final attempts were now made to sink them. The first took the shape of six 702 Ku Bettys tasked to attack individually in a series of sorties

planned by Lt Hada Kiyoshi. They were preceded by a search pair which left Vunakanau three minutes apart, commencing at 1655hrs. At 1845hrs, and groping through dark squalls, the first found a large flotilla of ships but no carriers. Working on the principle that this was a bird in the hand, it was decided to attack these, lest they be lost again in the marginal visibility. The first of Hada's torpedo-equipped Bettys accordingly left Vunakanau at 1957hrs; however, FCPO Miyahara Masakazu pulled his bomber from the mission after becoming lost. The last Betty left at 2150hrs. The radar aboard USS *Essex* tracked these five individual Bettys as they approached, two of which closed to within 25 nautical miles. The ship's log records: "The enemy was combing the area in which we were attacked in order to launch a night torpedo attack. It is believed possible that these bogeys failed to detect TF50.3 because other bogeys to the north contacted TF39 and reported their contact to the night torpedo planes."

The last of these pesky Bettys returned early next morning at 0020hrs, and claim to have hit three ships, but no torpedo found its mark. They had in fact attacked three ships of TF39 led by cruiser USS *Montpelier*, destroyers USS *Charles Ausburne*, *Converse*, and *Spence*. These ships all fired at individual Betty intruders, commencing at 1917hrs, which were dropping torpedoes and red flares, but registering no hits. In fact the American's ship-borne AA guns lightly damaged three of Hada's Bettys. However, there was also an ominous occurrence. At 1957hrs USS *Spence* logged an "underwater jolt from an unknown source." Was this a near-miss from a torpedo?

In the interim, the second attempt to find the carriers was planned by senior 751 Ku officer Lt-Cdr Adachi Jiro – another five Bettys were sortied to scour the area separately and hit the carriers. The efforts of these Bettys, with tail numbers 350, 352, 385, 376, and 381, proved even more futile than their 702 Ku counterparts before them, yet another instance when the parlous weather conditions thwarted best efforts. Despite his seniority, Adachi himself flew the first sortie in Betty 350, leaving Vunakanau at 1800hrs and returning to Vunakanau's cement runway the next morning at 0010hrs. In reality these six bombers meandered over an area long-evacuated by their enemy. The last Betty returned to Vunakanau the next morning at 0100hrs.

Parafragmentation bombs spill over Vunakanau's revetments during a low-level raid where 702 Ku Betty bombers are parked. These revetments were built from concrete blocks.

A final attempt was now made with four torpedo-toting Kates (two *Shokaku*, two *Zuikaku*) led by redoubtable *Shokaku* officer Lt Ono Hiroji, flying as an observer. There is symmetry that this last Kate mission was led by the same officer who had led the first Kate mission of Operation *Ro-Go* on November 2. Ono's quartet departed Vunakanau at 1825hrs and scoured the dark seas in formation for just over five hours, finding nothing, and all landing back at Vunakanau at 2335hrs.

Ono's best efforts and that of the Bettys marked the de facto end of Operation *Ro-Go*. That evening, Commander of the Combined Fleet, Admiral Koga Mineichi, mulled over the grievous loss reports of the November 11 carrier aircraft. If losses continued apace, his fleet air resources would be severely weakened. The next morning he issued two key orders: all remaining cruisers were to leave Rabaul, and the majority of the surviving carrier aircraft were to return to Truk. These flew out of Rabaul commencing departure at 0800hrs the next day, November 13, for the long overwater ferry flight back to Truk. As a compromise to defending Rabaul, Koga authorized a detachment from *Zuikaku* to remain in Rabaul until January 1944.

Nonetheless, the combined outcome of the two USN carrier strikes against Rabaul meant that USN warships now controlled Solomons waters. And, the landing at Torokina proceeded steadily to build the massive airfield complex sought by US air power. Thus grew a considerable base and complex from which Rabaul would be pounded in the forthcoming months. Operation *Ro-Go*, in every sense, had failed to meet even one of its objectives.

AFTERMATH AND ANALYSIS

Of course, Japanese attempts to prevent the northern Solomons advance did not stop with the cessation of Operation *Ro-Go*. In the weeks following, attacks continued to be made by Rabaul's land-based units and floatplanes against US shipping and landing forces around the Treasury Islands, Torokina, and Bougainville waters in general. With the withdrawal of most carrier resources back to Truk, and in the light of the disproportionate number of a total of 38 Vals lost in the operation, it was decided to reinforce Rabaul's dive-bombers.

On November 15, 26 brand-new D3A2 Model 22 Vals from 552 Ku (two dozen plus two spares) were transferred to Rabaul from the Marshall Islands led by commander Captain Tanaka Yoshio. The Vals were shipped to Truk then flown down to Rabaul. Upon arrival, a detachment was briefly stationed at Kavieng, while the group went through area familiarization and training. It flew its first mission from Rabaul on December 3. However, inexperience was evident in its aircrew ranks; for a start, its *hikotaicho* was a reserve lieutenant who had arrived in the Marshalls on November 5, Hayashibara Moto'o. The December 1943 Allied landing at Arawe in Western New Britain saw the unit urgently pressed into action alongside the Vals from 582 Ku. To ease space restrictions at Vunakanau, the unit's entire aircraft complement moved to Kerevat airfield near Rabaul on December 18 – an airfield that suffered considerable drainage challenges. The Arawe campaign saw 552 Ku incur tremendous losses and, with almost no Vals left to fly, the unit ceased operations on January 25, 1944.

The capricious weather which had dogged Operation *Ro-Go* throughout continued to hamper Japanese efforts for the next few weeks, made mainly at night, as losses from daylight missions would have been prohibitive. Then, within the fortnight, a flotilla of USN destroyers intercepted a Japanese supply run to Bougainville. A sea battle fought just south of Cape St. George saw three Japanese destroyers sunk with no damage to the American ships. Rabaul's role as a major naval base had drawn to a close.

Throughout the remainder of 1943 and then into 1944, Allied air power continued to pound Buin, Buka, Ballale, and Tonolei Harbor. Continuous CAPs maintained air

The wreckage of a G4M1 Betty bomber washed up upon a South Seas coastline.

Engineers service a reconnaissance D4Y1-C at Lakunai during Operation *Ro-Go*. Dzus fasteners on the access panel have been removed to access the oil intercooler while an engineer adjusts clearance on the retractable cowl. The reconnaissance version retained an optical gun sight as seen here.

supremacy over Torokina, while the complex was expanded and consolidated, finally seeing it used as a major fighter and logistical base from which to assault Rabaul. This expanding supremacy also made it increasingly difficult for Japanese reconnaissance aircraft to operate with impunity. Torokina would be used by aircraft striking Rabaul directly, and then targets in Bougainville, for the war's remainder.

By themselves, the numbers of losses the Japanese sustained during Operation *Ro-Go* in some respects present only superficial analysis yet were so severe that closer examination is justified. Of the 173 carrier aircraft flown down from Truk on November 1, only 53 returned there on November 13, thus incurring a terrible loss rate of 70 percent. The inventory breakdown is 42 lost from 82 Zero-sen, 38 of 45 Vals, 34 of 40 Kates, and all six D4Y1-C Judy reconnaissance aircraft. Furthermore, 192 carrier-based aircrew had arrived from Truk, of which 86 had lost their lives during Operation *Ro-Go*. An astute observer will notice this figure does not align with the number/type of carrier aircraft lost, as many Vals and Kates operated with observers and navigators furnished by land-based units.

Furthermore, an imperative factor during the operation – morale – remained in low ebb throughout. The combination of gloomy morale and low experience levels among aircrews was recognized only too well by the Japanese themselves, summarized in one post-war critique: "The skill of the pilots and crew members was considerably inferior compared to that of the Munda operation. Furthermore a considerable number of young and inexperienced pilots were among the flight personnel of the task force which participated in Operation *Ro-Go*, thus good results were unattainable."

A salient fact is that the Allies were unaware that there were nearly 63,000 Japanese on Bougainville when they planned the Torokina landing, nearly four times what they assessed, in fact. The Japanese Army did not counterattack Torokina with ground forces until early March 1944, in a brief but bloody campaign which lasted only several days. Having secured neither victory nor gain, the IJA then withdrew, leaving thousands of dead

Civilian nurse Miss Watanabe Shizu tends wounded Japanese IJN personnel on the veranda of the 8th Fleet Navy Hospital at Namanula, Rabaul, late 1943.

behind. Afterwards the American forces remained ensconced in Torokina's secure perimeter and as a strategy let the Japanese "wither on the vine." The three major airfields constructed at Torokina continued to expand with impunity, with numerous cantonment and supply depots later built.

At noon on November 13, command of the Torokina landing passed from commander of TF31, Rear Admiral Theodore "Ping" Wilkinson, to Major General Roy Geiger, commanding general of the First Marine Amphibious Corps. In the interim, TF31 continued to furnish naval and logistical support.

Much positive publicity ensued in the US following the Fifth Air Force November 2, 1943 raid. However, if aerial combat is considered a gauge of success, then "Bloody Tuesday" was instead a Japanese victory. Allied intelligence was unaware of the carrier resources flown into Rabaul from Truk the previous day, and the USAAF aircrews were surprised at the ferocity and strength of aerial resistance. The unexpected Japanese fighter defense produced chaotic scrambles for both carrier and land-based fighters, creating turmoil at the three airfields of Vunakanau, Lakunai, and Rapopo. A host of takeoff accidents temporarily grounded many fighters when they were needed most.

The aftermath of this raid was a bizarre US publicity campaign. On November 29, the cover of the magazine *Life* published a dramatic photograph of a Mitchell bomber flying low over Rabaul harbor. The associated caption stated that the October–November 1943 series of USAAF Rabaul raids had destroyed 140 vessels and 700 aircraft. These overwhelming figures were sourced back to a press briefing which had been held in Brisbane three weeks earlier by a member of General MacArthur's staff. The US Army briefing officer stated that in nine major Rabaul raids conducted between October 10 and November 2, 732 Japanese aircraft had been destroyed or damaged, along with 138 vessels destroyed. In fact, only one destroyer had been sunk at Rabaul by the USAAF in this period, with perhaps 40 aircraft destroyed. Furthermore, most shipping damage had been done instead by the USN November 5 raid, and repair units at Vunakanau, working around the clock, had rendered airworthy many bomb-damaged airframes.

Such hyperbole laid fertile ground for criticism of MacArthur on the basis that he deliberately exaggerated enemy strength and losses while minimizing his own. Many claimed

Lt J. E. Lockridge in the cockpit of VF-34 Hellcat #117 at Turtle Bay on Espiritu Santo. This squadron flew its first mission on March 7, 1944 from Piva Yoke, one of the major airfields built following the Torokina invasion.

such policy damaged domestic morale when it was clear that these wild overestimations enjoyed official endorsement. The myth continued to be perpetuated when in 1949 former Fifth Air Force Commander General George Kenney wrote of the November 2 raid, "Never in the long history of warfare had so much destruction been wrought upon the forces of a belligerent nation so swiftly and at such little cost."

The neutralization and isolation of Rabaul ultimately proved disastrous for the Japanese. USMC and Thirteenth Air Force air units continued to pummel Rabaul throughout the first half of 1944, then eased off with isolated attacks, the last of which took place on August 8, 1945. Its isolation meant that its substantive garrison which, by way of contrast, outnumbered the defenders of Okinawa, had become de facto POWs. A massive system of underground tunnels was constructed mostly with POW labor. This system, combined with the cultivation of widespread self-sustaining gardens, saw the garrison retire from combat in reasonable comfort.

Following the unsuccessful attempts to prove itself as a torpedo bomber, RAAF Beaufort squadrons were increasingly withdrawn from front-line duties. By 1945, they were confined to the rear echelon New Guinea base of Tadji, flying routine but sometimes costly missions against isolated garrisons.

A limited number of submarine supply runs down to Bougainville from Rabaul ceased in April 1944. These brought limited supplies and also evacuated only officer pilots. Right through until war's end a regular air service existed between Rabaul and Buin, flown at night by Jake floatplanes of the 105 Base Unit during full moon periods. These brought limited medical supplies and evacuated several officers. Two Combined Fleet Mavis flying boats visited Buka at night from Truk, one in June 1944 and the last in April 1945. The 17th Army commander Lieutenant General Hyakutake Haruyoshi suffered a stroke in February 1945. An attempt to evacuate him by air was unsuccessful as he could not be laid down as a stretcher patient, so he remained on Erventa Island.

By early 1944 the IJA 6th Division around southern Bougainville had all but retired from combat. A captured POW in 1945 reported that since June 1944 about 70 percent of the army was engaged full-time in gardening duties around Buin, then went on to say:

After the Torokina offensive, the daily ration of rice was reduced to 50 grams for the whole of Bougainville. Not all troops in rear areas were given as much, but some front line units received about 300 grams per day. Except for front line troops, all other soldiers have been living exclusively on their garden produce for many months, with occasional minimal rations of rice and bean paste.

Being part of New Guinea meant Rabaul and surrounding areas including Bougainville fell under Australian political authority, thus behoving Australian military forces to accept Rabaul's surrender. After an unimaginable amount of wartime action around Rabaul, it is ironic that a diminutive World War I destroyer named HMS *Vendetta* arranged the surrender. It entered Simpson Harbour on September 4, 1945. It is fitting that the Japanese delegation to organize matters was led by an air staff officer of the 11th Air Fleet, Captain Sanagi

Staff officer in the 11th Air Fleet, Captain Sanagi Takeshi (circled) signs the document which has just organized Rabaul's surrender in two days' time. This photo was taken aboard destroyer HMS *Vendetta* on September 4, 1945. Sanagi has just signed the agreement while Australian Brigadier General Edward Sheehan (circled) is about to.

Takeshi. Prior to being posted to Rabaul in 1943, Sanagi had headed an operations team at Imperial IJN headquarters in Tokyo. Aboard the destroyer, Sanagi negotiated with the most senior Australian representative, Brigadier General Edward Sheehan, also a staff officer. Discussion which commenced uneasily terminated with agreement to set the surrender ceremony two days hence.

On September 6 the formal surrender was signed on behalf of the IJA by General Imamura Hitoshi, while the IJN forces were surrendered by Admiral Kusaka Jinichi. The ceremony was held on the flight deck of light carrier HMS *Glory* in Simpson Harbour, authorized by the signatures of these two senior officers. Kusaka used his own personal ink and pen to script his name in Kanji, while Imamura surrendered his sword as requested by the Australians. The surrender document outlined the capitulation of 139,300 military and civilian Japanese throughout New Britain (89,000), New Ireland (12,600), Bougainville (23,400), and New Guinea (14,300).

These numbers were nearly five times what the Australians had expected. With too many POWs to supervise, the Australians disarmed the Japanese garrisons, then ordered the Japanese officers to organize self-sufficient camps until they could be repatriated. For the Japanese this meant business as usual; cached food stocks and widespread field cultivation helped feed the large garrison. Due to the lack of shipping, repatriation did not begin until May 1946 and took five months to complete. Meanwhile, General Imamura busied himself planning an education policy for the projected timeframe in captivity. His guidance defined camp life routine in which he robustly promoted education programs for all POWs.

Japanese officers were tasked to develop curricula, compiling textbooks and giving lectures. A dedicated education unit was formed, No. 12 Education Group, ordering that compulsory subjects be taught in the morning, and electives in the evening. Subjects pertaining to self-sufficiency were compulsory, and vocational subjects were designed for those with only primary school level. These courses aimed to help soldiers acquire skills which would facilitate their post-war employment. This preparation for the return to civilian life redirected the residual militaristic spirit of the Japanese servicemen toward education. It restored their pride, particularly for those who had received no chance to engage in combat before the surrender.

Japanese POWs discuss the distribution of food at one of the Rabaul camps in October 1945.

There were thousands of stranded Japanese outside Rabaul too. An example is the camp established at Kareki on the island of Fauro, southeast of Bougainville, during November 1945. The Australian 7th Infantry Battalion moved 28,000 Japanese soldiers from the Buin area and other parts of southern Bougainville and the Shortlands to Kareki in order to concentrate all POWs from the region into one location. Here the Japanese worked as laborers on infrastructure projects until late January 1946, when they were repatriated to Japan aboard carrier *Hosho*. The water system they constructed is still used today.

The eventual surrender of Rabaul was similar to the isolation of Wewak, both effected primarily by air power, isolating major strongholds to the point where occupation by ground forces was unnecessary. The key to achieving air superiority was having effective and high-performance fighters. As the Solomons campaign increasingly encroached upon Rabaul, in some respects the Zero-sen fell short of its US counterparts. A new generation of American fighters, including the F4U Corsair and F6F Hellcat, offered superior armament and high-altitude performance. However, the one advantage the Zero-sen never conceded was its maneuverability at lower levels. With the benefit of hindsight, we can see that post-war accounts exaggerate the success of these new Allied types against the Zero in the South Seas campaigns; however, the reality is that it more than held its own, right up until the last major aerial battles over Rabaul in February 1944.

Allied planners knew that moving airfields close enough to Rabaul permitted these short-range and robust single-engine fighters to reach Rabaul. Supporting the logistics to capture and secure territory in addition to maintaining supply chains meant building a logistical army which US forces pulled off masterfully. By way of contrast, the Japanese placed less emphasis on logistical manpower, plant equipment, and maintenance. The Japanese also settled for second-rate construction; much was done by POWs, who were forced to work and whose health and strength were compromised by a substandard diet. Petty sabotage was rampant, and supplies were often stored where convenient, rather than strategically placed. Several cantonment areas were left unprotected. Several missions were delayed when torpedoes had to be driven between airfields on the backs of underpowered Isuzu trucks on rutted roads. Similar inefficiencies extended to the entire Japanese manufacturing chain, which was overwhelmed, unbalanced, and inefficient.

A major turning point was reached by Halsey's committed air strikes against Rabaul's ships on November 5, then the follow-up raid six days later on November 11. Had the Japanese cruisers sortied from Simpson Harbour on the evening of November 5, the US invasion fleet at Torokina would likely have been wiped out, and the Marines pushed off the beachhead. The loss would have delayed construction of the airfields at Torokina and later occupation of the Green Islands, and would have discouraged landings on New Britain. The bitter truth is that the Fifth Air Force New Guinea air campaigns were devastating against Wewak, but achieved little against Rabaul.

In the middle of all this, and despite resolute intention, Operation *Ro-Go*'s contribution toward halting the US advances in the theater and against Rabaul was virtually negligible. In the end, the campaign failed to achieve any of its objectives. Poignantly, the failure of Operation *Ro-Go* highlights the massive disparity between the size and capability of US and Japanese forces which had been building steadily over 1943.

FURTHER READING

Regrettably, there are no accounts of the Pacific War pertaining to the Operation *Ro-Go* era which accurately source the Japanese side of events. The language barrier is as formidable today as it was back in World War II, so it seems. Thus, most English language books about the late 1943 Pacific air war are unbalanced at best, wrong at worst, as they fail to consult primary Japanese sources. The same books continue to quote Allied claims which are overinflated and/or inaccurate.

However, Bruce Gamble's *Rabaul* trilogy does the era justice, and for the earlier Pacific War era Peter Ingman's *South Pacific Air War* volumes accurately cite and balance the Japanese side too. The recollections of Fifth Air Force Commander Major General George Kenney contained in "General Kenney Reports: A Personal History of the Pacific War" are priceless. His more extravagant claims aside, one can nevertheless sense the reality of the times and the know-how which so drove his initiatives. Other books relevant to the era are:

Claringbould, Michael, *Operation I-Go: Yamamoto's Last Offensive*, Avonmore Books, 2020
Hickey, Lawrence, *Warpath Across the Pacific*, IRP, 1984
Morison, Samuel Eliot, *Breaking the Bismarcks Barrier* (USN Operations in WW2, Vol. 6, 1952)
Sakaida, Henry, *The Siege of Rabaul*, Phalanx Publishing, 1996
Shaw, Henry Jr., and Kane, Douglas, *Isolation of Rabaul: History of USMC Operations in WW2*, Vol. I, 2013

This particular Osprey title book only cites primary sources and official histories.

US sources are confined to all relevant ships' logs, action reports, official diaries, summary reports, air unit histories, and air unit reports. Curiously, several key documents are missing, including several USS *Saratoga* action reports.

Japanese Sources

Diaries/POW interrogation reports of pilots (various units): Tanaguchi Masayoshi, Yoshida Masa'aki, Muraoka Shinichi, Shimizu Kazuo, Katsuaki Kira, Kimura Toshio, Hasegawa Tomoari. Memoirs of 582 Ku Zero-sen pilot WO Tsunoda Kazuo, 582 Ku pilot FPO2c Nakagawa Matao, 204 Ku pilot Leading Aircraftsman Kato Masao, 705 Ku Betty crew Matsuo Yasuo, Sakagawa Bun, and Yonekura Shiro.

Radio Tokyo transcripts, 1943
Otaka Nakajima, *The Pacific War as Viewed from Combined Fleet Operations Room*
Tokuki Matsuda, *Kakuta Kakuji: The Warrior Who Pushes Through the Enemy*, PHP Bunko, 2009
Meiji Centennial Series (Vol. 74), *History of the Naval Academy*, Hara Shobo
Memoirs of Lt-Cdr Okumiya Masatake, staff officer to Rear Admiral Kakuta Kakuji
Diary of Rear Admiral Sanwa Yoshiwa, Chief of Staff (aviation), Southeast Area Fleet
Diary of Vice Admiral Kusaka Jinichi, Commander SE Area Fleet – privately hand-written (Oct.– Nov. 1943)
Manual of Military Secret Orders ATIS, captured document, dated July 20, 1943
Japanese Air Terms in Kanji, Squadron Leader A. R Boyce, Far Eastern Bureau, Calcutta, 1944
Historical Monograph Series, "Summary of aerial operations in New Guinea late 1943 by Japanese High Command," Southeast Naval Operations, Part 4
Translation of Japanese Navy messages, Japanese Naval Forces, Sep.–Dec. 1943
Tabulated Records of Movement (TROMs) for relevant Japanese ships cited in text

Japanese Newspapers

Japan Times and Advertiser, articles September to December 1943
Asahi Shimbun, articles September to December 1943

Unit operations logs (*kodochosho*) – handwritten in Kanji and Katakana
No. 201 Kokutai, 204 Kokutai, 252 Kokutai, 253 Kokutai, 251 Kokutai, 582 Kokutai, 751 Kokutai, 204 Kokutai unofficial history (post-war, compiled by veterans), 501 Kokutai, 552 Kokutai, 702 Kokutai, 938 Kokutai, 958 Kokutai, *kodochosho* for *Zuikaku*, *Shokaku*, and *Zuiho* for relevant timeframes.

Ship operations logs (*sentochosho*) and Tabulated Records of Movements (TROMs) for all relevant Japanese ships
Senshi Sosho Vol. 96 Nanto Homen Kaigun Sakusen
Gatto Tesshu Go, Southeastern Area Naval Operations

INDEX

Note: page numbers in **bold** refer to illustrations, captions and plates.